Boom Town Reflections

I0559387

Volume – 4

A NEW BEGINNING

Mark A. Gregg

4900 California Ave, Bakersfield, CA 93309,
USA
Collins's website address:
www.collinspublishinghouse.com
First published in English by Collins Publishing
House in 2024
1st Edition 2024
Mark A. Gregg © 2024
Mark A. Gregg asserts the moral right
to be identified as the author of this work.
A catalogue record for this book is available
from the Library of Congress United States.
E Book ISBN: 978-1-966029-20-5
Paperback ISBN: 978-1-966029-21-2
Hardcover ISBN: 978-1-966029-22-9
Printed and bounded in United States of
America.
For permission requests, contact
info@collinspublishinghouse.com

Author's Dedication

This book is dedicated to the memory of Orville (Bert) Donovan (June 7, 1934 ~ August 21, 2021). A mentor who taught me a tremendous amount about power plants and a man who went out of his way (more than once!) to keep me employed inspite of my many bad decisions. *Thanks again, Bert!*

Table of Contents

CHAPTER 1
WHEATLAND, WYOMING.

Have you ever considered how handy a time-machine would be? *Seriously.* The ability to roll-back time without losing the memory of lessons learned would be monumental for most people.

Unfortunately, I didn't have a time-machine, but I did have an intense, unshakable memory of my massive failures in Farmington, New Mexico. These memories would haunt me for years. They were personal failures and extreme and costly professional failures.

The damage I inflicted on the mighty Four Corners Power Plant was inexcusable. My intense drive to become a Control Room Operator threw common sense, logic, and reasoning out the window. I now understood that holding a job title did not mean you earned it or *even had a clue how to perform it.* I was the poster boy of incompetence and now every shred of my being wanted to rid myself of this self-imposed black cloud of existence I was living for the past year.

Fortunately, our time in Farmington had a silver lining. I had yet to realize just how bright and amazing that lining was. I was supernaturally delivered from alcohol addiction. No, it wasn't through or by a Church or Pastor or any program whatsoever. We never attended Church in Farmington. Not once. We certainly didn't hang with Church people in Farmington. In fact, *we didn't even know any Church people in Farmington.*

What I needed to realize is the God of the universe touched me and set me on a path that was irreversible. Getting hired at the Laramie River Station was a tremendous blessing, but I didn't have a clue what was in store for us when I accepted the Control Room Operator job at the new, three-unit Laramie River Station in Wheatland, Wyoming.

The actual move from Farmington to Wheatland was a joy. Basin Electric paid the moving company to handle everything. This included packing our household goods, loading them in the truck, and unloading them in Wheatland. They even paid us a mileage benefit for driving our car and paid for the hotels along the way. *We felt nothing short of royalty.*

We splurged by spending almost $30.00 to lodge ourselves in a Ramada Inn the first night in Pueblo, Colorado. It was wonderful to finally stay in a higher-end hotel without worrying about the expense, or wondering if critters of the creepy-crawly nature were sharing the bed with us.

While the December weather was crisp, we missed major blizzards and other weather mishaps while enjoying the drive to our new home. Brandi was 2 ½ years old now and quite active. However, she made surprisingly little fuss during the entire trek to Wheatland. It was as if she was as pleased to leave Farmington as Vangie and I.

We arrived in Wheatland content and excited about a new start without the excess baggage I carried at Four Corners. Unfortunately, and not surprisingly, Wheatland was seriously afflicted with boom town syndrome. Initially, we were very naïve about the level of human suffering seething below the surface of this bustling construction-ravaged village.

The degree of human suffering from substance abuse and poor decisions always multiplies in boom towns. Maybe it was the temporary nature of the nomadic lifestyle or simply the rapid concentration of fortune seekers selfishly competing for as much as they could gather in a short period.

Boom towns were a petri dish of humanity. Fortunately, they cultured some good as well as the bad. We saw our share of both as time progressed. Besides boom town syndrome, Wheatland experienced some particularly vexing weather challenges.

The cold and relentless Wyoming wind scoured the streets of dust and trash only to immediately supply suitable replacements. You either acclimated to the wind or succumbed to it due to depression, self-medication, or worse. Like any boom town, the suicide rate was much higher than the national average.

It was common to hear about people leaving, citing their dislike of the wind. I didn't mind the wind nearly as much as Vangie. She loathed the continuous buffeting of the trailer and the harsh assault on your well-being when outdoors. Letting a small child or animal out of the house was always a difficult decision. You were constantly worried about them blowing down the street as they were engulfed in violent, abrasive wind gusts.

Thousands of construction workers seemed to look forward to the inevitable loss of jobs and receiving the prize of... *Moving elsewhere*. A commonly heard statement among the construction personnel was, "There are only two good construction jobs... The one you just left and the one you are going to." As time progressed, I came to understand this deep in my core. The inevitable truisms of life are sometimes hidden in humorous adages such as this.

Our trailer on 2157 West Basin Street in the sprawling Black Mountain Village was much nicer and certainly higher quality than the one in Rock Springs. Many of the Basin Electric employees were underwhelmed with their lodging choices by Basin Electric when first transitioning to the area. We weren't. Compared to what we experienced in Rock Springs, the Basin trailers were veritable châteaus.

The Basin Electric trailers were livable and even comfortable if you were honest with yourself and allowed them to be. Regardless, the goal of every Basin Electric employee was to eventually find a "real" home outside of Black Mountain Village.

Our three-bedroom model allowed us to use the master bedroom in the front of the trailer while delegating the middle bedroom for Brandi and the very back bedroom for storage. In our six years of marriage, we accumulated more junk than could be shoved into a 14' x 80' trailer house.

The *"storage bedroom"* was our first crisis arriving in Wheatland. It seems the movers stealthily relieved us of a silver dollar collection generously given by Grandad Stringer. The movers then made up for it by packing a 10-pound bag of potatoes in a cardboard box with an uninspiring tiffany lamp. This nasty box was buried in the middle of the room and was stacked almost to the ceiling. Several weeks into our tenure in Wheatland, the smell coming from that bedroom was egregiously putrid.

When we could no longer stomach the odor with the door tightly closed (and a towel shoved underneath), we begrudgingly unloaded the bedroom to find a cardboard box with a liquified bottom, courtesy of the rotting potatoes. The incredibly foul witch's brew produced by the decomposing potatoes soaked through the box and into the carpet on the bedroom floor.

Cleaning up this mess was virtually impossible. The carpet was permanently etched with a faint but noticeable stink. We didn't realize the silver dollar collection was missing until we moved to our new house several months later. It was gone forever with no available recourse.

There were two food stores in Wheatland in 1978. A bright new, relatively large Safeway store on the west side of town just off Interstate – 25, and a small, dark, older Jack and Jill store in downtown Wheatland. A single-screen cinema was across the street to the south of the Jack and Jill food store. There were a few clothing stores, including a Golden Rule store. This was the forerunner to the J.C. Penney chain and, for some reason, still bore the Golden Rule moniker instead of J.C. Penney. It probably had to do with it being very old, dark, and small. Unfortunately, driving through the streets of Wheatland in 1979 evoked pictures of the great depression. It appeared that minimal change had occurred in this small village since the 1930's.

The oft-needed respite in Wheatland was the eternal hope and temporary relief of a trip to Cheyenne for groceries, clothes, or just to have dinner in a real restaurant. Wheatland's indulgent culinary offerings consisted of Vimbos, Breakfast Inn, Taco Johns, and Pizza Hut.

Vimbos was an aging, two-story cinderblock hotel that provided restaurant meals to weary travelers for many years prior to the arrival of the power plant. Vimbo's contribution to the gastronomical landscape was a bland offering of comfort cuisine, seasoned by a shortage of cooks because they could make twice the money being laborers at the power plant.

It is my belief that the "chef du jour" at Vimbos was changed almost weekly, and employment in this prestigious role was not particularly contingent upon previous cooking experience or possibly even a heartbeat.

Pizza Hut and Taco Johns were the primary dining establishments, but Vimbos was acceptable for Church-going people who desired a large Sunday meal if you could not swing a trip to Cheyenne. When Cheyenne became fatiguing, you could always drive another 45 minutes to Fort Collins, Colorado.

Shortly after arriving in Wheatland, we purchased a seriously battered 1969, ¾ ton Chevy pick-up from a farmer in the area. We needed two vehicles because I was on a straight dayshift (everyone was in the initial months). I felt that a pick-up truck was essential to life.

In recent years, the farmer used this beat-up wreck as a beast of burden for fencing and other chores. By the looks of it, possibly even a demolition derby or two. The truck was primarily red but was beaten to pieces. It appeared that every square inch of the body, bed, and cab was dinged, dented, and molested in some form or fashion. However, it ran surprisingly well.

I cleaned years of mud, fertilizer, and miscellaneous schmutz from inside the cab before it became our backup transportation. It was only used if Vangie needed the Pinto while I was at work. At that time, I had no idea the trouble that red heap of junkyard fodder was bringing with it.

About a week after purchasing the truck, an uptight, local Wheatland police officer knocked on our trailer door. It was early evening. He was a pugnacious, heavy-set local hack that seemed very intense for a country boy. I answered the door, surprised at seeing a cop. He immediately took control of the situation as the door opened.

"Are you the owner of this pick-up?" He turned and pointed at the battered, red hulk in the driveway.

"Yes, I am, why do you ask?" I was genuinely curious.

"I will cut to the chase; I want you to pay for the stop sign you knocked down, and we can avoid the legalities." He stared at me intensely with malice in his eyes.

I was stunned at his opening volley. "I have no idea what you are talking about," I stated, blown away by his fervor.

"Let's not play games. We both know you were in this truck and knocked down the stop sign at the corner of South Street and 24th last night." His intensity was intimidating.

I answered defensively, "I was home all evening. I haven't driven this truck in a couple of days."

"Fine, I'll play along." His gall was scary. "Who, then, borrowed the truck last night?"

"That truck has not moved in over two days. No one has driven it." Anger was now welling up inside of me.

"Look, we can save the city money and you a heap of trouble if you just pay for the damn stop sign that was knocked over. I hope you fully appreciate that I am cutting you slack." He paused for a moment. "Please understand I don't have to do this for you."

"What is your name?" I asked, trying to suppress my anger.

"Officer Corte of the Wheatland Police Department." I could now sense anger in *his* voice.

"Officer Corte, you have the wrong truck and the wrong person. I am telling you, this truck has not been started or moved in at least two days. If your stop sign was knocked down last night, it was some other red truck, not this one."

"Fine." His voice was resolute. "If you want to play it this way, I will have to charge you with leaving the scene of an accident. When you are found guilty, it will be on your record permanently and probably cost you a large fine, possibly even a jail sentence." My heart skipped a beat. ***This guy was deadly serious about this.***

"First, I don't have a record because I have never had a run-in with the law." I paused and drew a breath. "Do you have a witness or evidence supporting your charge?" My thoughts were racing. Vangie moved closer to the door to hear what Officer Corte was saying.

"I have the signpost that perfectly matches your truck's paint. The tire tracks look like the tires on your truck. Unless you have hard proof that you and your truck have not moved, I have all the evidence I need to charge you." He was not backing off in the least. I could not believe this was happening.

"Look, I bought that truck in the exact shape it is currently in. It was a local farm truck and was beat-up exactly as it looks now when I purchased it. If I hit your stop-sign, I would have called the police and filed a report. I am telling you that I did not hit your sign. That truck has not moved in a couple of days!" My patience was almost depleted.

"Very well. I gave you a chance. All I want is the stop sign paid for, and life will go well for you." He stopped, looked back at the truck, and then looked into my eyes. "I am giving you a day to think about what I am offering before filing charges. Maybe you should even talk to an attorney. He will tell you that what I am offering is far easier and cheaper than the alternative."

We stood awkwardly, eye to eye for a moment before he continued. "I will see you tomorrow afternoon at about this same time. I hope you let common sense prevail, otherwise, you will be in some serious trouble." He turned and walked quickly to his police car sitting at the curb.

"That's nuts!" Vangie exclaimed as I shut the door. "Why would he do this?"

"He seems to truly believe I knocked the stop sign down." I was perplexed and anxious.

"What are you going to do?" Vangie's voice was now angry.

"I don't know. The intersection he is talking about is up and around the corner. It is too dark to see anything tonight." I looked at the clock on the wall. "I will ask for some time off in the morning to straighten this out."

The next morning, I got up early and drove the pickup over to the corner where the stop sign was assaulted. Sure enough, it was broken off about midway down the wooden post. Red paint was on the jagged portion of the signpost that was lying at a 45° angle. There were also black skid marks where the offending vehicle apparently locked the brakes, trying to miss the sign.

It didn't take me long to realize that the skid marks were far too narrow to be my 3/4 ton pickup. I ran back home and got a tape measure and a camera. I clumsily measured the width of the skid marks, trying to snap a picture of the measurement. I then measured the width of the tires on the truck. They were about 6" wider than the skid marks fading into the roadbed.

I knew the skid marks wouldn't last for a legal battle, so I decided to get as much help as possible. I started knocking on the trailer doors near the intersection. I found two housewives, both much older than me, who agreed to come outside and witness me measuring the width of the skid marks. I explained to both ladies what was happening. Apparently, it invoked empathy for my situation with them agreeing to be witnesses.

In those days, the only instant pictures were from a Polaroid camera. They were expensive to purchase, and the film was very costly. Like us, most people owned cheap Kodak Instamatic cameras that required the film to be sent to a lab somewhere, developed, and then returned. Usually, it was a 3 - or 4 - day process. Much larger towns had one-hour film development at specialty camera shops, but this service was unavailable in Wheatland.

After dropping the film at Safeway, I went to the Wheatland Police Station and asked to speak to Officer Corte. The receptionist at the front desk said that he was not on shift yet. I then asked to speak to the police chief. She took my personal information and went into another office, closing the door behind her. A few minutes later, the Wheatland Police Chief came out and greeted me.

I told him my story and assured him the pictures of the skid marks and the ladies who helped me would be available in a few days and asked if they could hold off filing charges. With raised eyebrows, he assured me they would not file charges and Officer Corte would not bother me again, but he wanted to see the pictures. He seemed like a reasonable guy and was far less intense than Corte was.

A few days later, after the developed pictures arrived back at Safeway, I dropped off a couple of clear ones showing the skid marks and the measurements. It was the last I ever heard about this from anyone. While I occasionally saw Officer Corte around town, I never talked to him again. I am guessing it was because the Police Chief intervened in this situation. Further, I never heard from the Police Chief again, though I am certain he was given the pictures. It was the only encounter I ever experienced with the Police.

All in all, the once sleepy little town of Wheatland was now rife with growing pains from the continuous influx and outgo of construction workers. This small, sleepy burg with a Church on every corner now regularly dealt with barroom brawls, crime, and even an occasional murder. The townspeople and local officials were ill-prepared to handle the explosion of humanity caused by the massive plant construction effort. I knew construction would finish someday and the town would eventually be a decent place to raise kids. My utter and complete focus was now on that gargantuan, imposing power plant with its 600' stacks sitting majestically outside of town.

CHAPTER 2
AN INCREDIBLE POWER PLANT

February 12th, 1979, was a momentous day for me. It was my first day of a brand-new life. I was now a control room operator without my reputation and failures dogging after me. The original 8 Laramie River Station control room operators met each other for the first time at the plant's front gate at 0800 Monday morning. Only three of us previously held the position of Control Room Operator. This made me feel better about my limited plant experience. Apparently, knowing that I held the title of Control Room Operator made me forget about the carnage I left behind at Four Corners.

Laramie River Station Circa 1982

The control room barely existed in the plant at this time. The control boards were covered with heavy, black plastic tarps (Visqueen) as construction personnel were still working on the walls and ceiling. It appeared to be a spectacular control room because the control boards were big, and there was an observation deck where people could look down into the control room. There was no expense being spared at this plant.

Babcock and Wilcox designed and built all three boilers, commonly known as B&W. All three turbines were designed and built by General Electric. Everything in the plant was uniform, big, bright, and, in my eyes, beautiful. All three units were equipped with state-of-the-art pollution control equipment for that era.

There's not much to say about the early days at the plant. We were on straight days and doing training every single day, ad-nauseum. This meant we were doing whatever we wanted in the guise of learning. We would trace pipes, albeit poorly, because so many systems were not complete.

Burns & McDonnell Engineering from Kansas City did the plant's design, engineering, and construction management. We all had a bad opinion of them because none of us possessed experience with this size of undertaking. 20/20 hindsight proved that Burns & McDonnell did an amazing job. So much so that many years later, I happily went to work for them. Unfortunately, during that time, we considered them idiots because *when ignorant people are overwhelmed by their circumstances, the easiest way to appear smart is to focus on someone else's faults.*

A few weeks into this process new operators began arriving regularly. We would hear their names bandied about and then, *Wham!* They were shaking your hand. LRS hired four operators from Southern California Edison. All four of them had excellent training but no coal-fired experience. This really didn't matter considering this was a new plant, and we were all going to learn as we started it up. However, those of us with coal-fired experience carefully made it an issue because it was our duty to make them feel inferior. After all, this was a new plant and there would be a lot of promotions as the inevitable turnover occurred.

The in-plant electrical system at LRS was far more complex than most plants because this was the only plant in the United States that a unit could generate onto the east grid or west grid. This unique arrangement required an extremely complicated in-plant electrical system that prevented the two systems from inadvertently being tied together. This action would bring forth calamity to the power plant and potential death to anyone near the circuit breaker(s) that initiated the tie.

The Southern California Edison boys were far more electrically knowledgeable than anyone else hired at the plant. One of the operators hired from Southern Cal Ed, Gordon Keller, was immediately promoted to Shift Supervisor. A short time later, he took Bert's job as operations supervisor, and Bert moved up to operations superintendent. Gordon was the oldest of all the operators hired from Edison, probably about 45 years old. He was very sharp on the electrical systems and a pretty good man overall.

Another "Edison" hire was a gentleman named Milton Marquette. He was ten years older than me. He was ruggedly handsome, and Vangie always said he looked like the movie star Charles Bronson.

Milton started at the plant a few months after I did. He needed to sell his home in Buena Park, California, before his wife and three children could come to Wheatland. He was quiet but possessed a look of complete savvy about him. I met him on his first day at the plant. He sported an elusive smile and reserved demeanor. His eyes were powerful and penetrating. He was a deep thinker and appeared extremely intelligent. He would size up every person he met before conversing with them at any length. There was something about him I liked. I wasn't sure what it was yet.

After arriving in Wheatland, Vangie and I started attending the First Christian Church. It was an old cinder block building on 13th Street. The Pastor was a rough-hewn Wyoming cowboy named Dan Barlow. Even though he was probably in his early 30s, he was an old soul, always speaking slowly and laboriously. He was likable but could bore the socks off a person wearing tight boots.

A few weeks after Milton Marquette started at the plant, Vangie and I were reticently attending Dan's Church. Much to my surprise, Milton was there. He was the only power plant person I saw at Church since moving to Wheatland. After the service I introduced him to Vangie, and she invited him to have Sunday dinner with us.

The dinner with Milt consisted of a simple red stew that Vangie made with V-8 Juice, meat, and vegetables. We found out over dinner that Milt and his wife Marie had been married for 11 years and had three children. Chad was the same age as Brandi, Kristi was 5, and Keri was 8. Milt's mom was Japanese and was still alive. Milt's Dad tragically died of a heart attack when Milt was 12 years old.

You could tell the memory of losing his dad carried a lot of pain. He had four siblings, two older sisters and two younger sisters, but no brothers. Milt and I hit it off right away. After spending the afternoon hearing about his family, Vangie and I looked forward to meeting Marie and their children.

At some point, the conversation drifted towards Church. He asked why we went to the Christian Church there in Wheatland. It was understood between us that the experience was a bit "painful." I told him we were there simply because I was baptized in a Christian Church and Vangie and I were married in the same Church. Simply put… *It was all we knew.*

He explained that they attended a Church called Melody Land in California and that it was an amazing Church. Milt spoke of it with extreme pride. Though he interviewed for the control room operator position here at LRS about the same time as me, he and Marie struggled to leave California primarily because of Church. This struggle is what, ultimately, delayed him from starting at LRS with the rest of us.

I thought this was odd. Why would Church be a major part of the decision to move to a new job? Ever since my experience at the river pump station at Four Corners, I was more attuned to spiritual matters, but I certainly would not use church as a factor in decision-making for a cross-country move. One of the many things we learned about Milton that afternoon was his sincerity.

Milt and I began to gravitate towards one another at the plant. He knew substantially more about power plants than I did. I learned a tremendous amount from him. I looked forward to these impromptu educational sessions and enjoyed his company greatly.

All in all, life at LRS was good but boring. You were surrounded by ongoing construction and half-finished systems. Nothing was running, and all there was to do was 'train, train, and train some more.' Depending on the person, this meant tracing pipes and looking at prints or simply sitting around complaining about Wheatland, the government, Bert Donovan, Wyoming, or anything else that happened to surface in day-to-day conversation.

One afternoon, several of us were sitting, grumbling, and conversing, mostly from sheer boredom because we were tired of the endless walking down of partially finished systems. I noticed that several of the operators, including Lorenzo Rodriguez one of the very savvy Southern California Edison hires, were discussing "chew", or chewing tobacco.

This was one of the most disgusting, nasty habits I ever observed. In some ways, "chew" is worse than smoking. While you may have to smell someone smoking, you couldn't 'un-see' these morons spitting their viscous, dark-brown, saliva-based pudding into coffee cups, pop cans, or directly into trash cans. The mess was everywhere. There were endless stories of people not paying attention and accidentally picking up a cup of someone's chew-spit, thinking it was their coffee, and then gagging as it hit their pallet.

I couldn't resist being in the conversation while they discussed the enjoyment and benefit of this vile, repulsive habit.

"Why do you put that crap in your mouths?" I asked with sheer disdain in my voice.

Lorenzo was the first to answer. "Have you ever tried it?" He was very outspoken and aggressive in most conversations.

"Do I look stupid?" I answered with equal aggression. They all started laughing.

"Do you really want me to answer that?" He retorted, laughing with the rest of them. I started laughing with them, realizing that I left myself wide open for ridicule.

"Here, put a small pinch in your lower lip." Lorenzo leaned forward and extended an open can of Copenhagen chewing tobacco. "I put a few drops of Southern Comfort in it to keep it good and moist." He then looked directly into my eyes and said, "Don't be ignorant and knock something you know absolutely nothing about. You are outnumbered by people who use it, so maybe we know something you don't".

The room went quiet, with all eyes staring expectantly at me. We squared off like two gunmen in an old black-and-white, western movie on TV. At that moment, his argument seemed quite valid. What could it hurt? At least I would have an idea of what they enjoyed about this disgusting, vile habit.

I put a pinch between my thumb and forefinger and carefully deposited it in my lower gum area in front of my bottom teeth. The flavor was not nearly as off-putting as I expected. In fact, it possessed a sweet, smoky essence to it. I nodded my head in indifference.

"See? Not so bad, is it?" Lorenzo chided.

"I guess not. I figured it tasted like it looked… Kind of like shit in a can." He and a few others laughed. I sucked on the mush in my lip for a few more minutes swallowing the juices.

The conversation drifted away from chewing tobacco to other equally important things when I began to feel dizzy and off-balance. A few minutes later, I began sweating profusely, and pressure began building in my stomach. The room was now spinning, and my hands were shaking violently. It only took a few more minutes to realize the contents of my stomach were soon to come forth, and my head was aching as badly as any migraine I ever experienced.

"Look, I think he's turning green!" One of the operators sitting next to me exclaimed loudly. Everyone in the room looked at me and broke out laughing hysterically. I was getting sicker by the moment. At that point, I knew I was going to heave, so I jumped up and ran to the restroom.

As soon as I entered the bathroom, I saw that my normally fish-belly white complexion was sallow, almost greenish, and my lips were a pale, sickly blue. I was so dizzy I could barely walk. The toilet was typically dirty, as most men's restrooms seemed to be. It didn't matter. I began violently wretching, painfully disgorging everything I had eaten in the last decade. It was horrible. I thought my entire GI tract was going to rip loose and spew out of my mouth. After a few minutes, I began to spastically dry-heave until I lost all strength and could barely stand on my feet.

I sat down on the toilet and, for the first time in my young life, knew what the prelude to death felt like. My body was shaking horribly, I was so dizzy I could barely sit straight, and I wanted it all to end. I thought about Vangie and Brandi, wondering if I would see them again. I don't think I ever felt that sick before or even after. After sitting in the stall for what seemed like hours, I heard someone walk into the restroom. Lorenzo's voice then hollered loudly.

"Mark… You in here?"

"Yeah," I replied weakly.

"You okay?" His mirth was barely disguised. You could tell he was trying not to outwardly laugh.

"Yeah, I'm fine." I could not even fake strength right now. I wanted to die and end it all.

"Just checking…" He then snickered, and I heard him leave the restroom.

I sat in the stall for almost an hour, slowly recovering from my trauma. When I felt strong enough to leave the restroom, I rode the elevator to the 14th floor, laboriously climbing the stairs to the roof of the plant.

Immersing myself in the vast Wyoming countryside refreshed me as the cool Wyoming breeze evaporated the sweat from my brow. I still felt terrible, but I learned several more important life lessons that day. I stayed on the roof until work was over and then quietly slinked to the parking lot, driving home to see my wife and child, whom I felt I almost abandoned that day.

Chapter 3
A Lifetime Friendship

There were several more weeks of the same routine at the plant. Watching the units slowly come together and become a semblance of a completed power plant was interesting.

Vangie was just starting to "show" now with a very small baby bump... *Oh, right.* I forgot to mention that January's in Wheatland were cold and windy. You remained indoors for a fair amount of time. Vangie was pregnant... Anyway, we were happy about it. It was a bit of a surprise but a welcome one.

Thankfully, she never experienced major issues with morning sickness when she carried Brandi three years earlier. Unfortunately, this was not the case with the new baby. She dealt with morning sickness late into the afternoon on many days. This new baby was kicking her butt. It was a rare day that Vangie did not wake up sick and felt terribly bad for a good part of the day. The Doctor gave her medication that helped. However, she still felt terrible much of the time. Fortunately, she was up and around the day Marie Marquette and her kids arrived in Wheatland.

The first time we saw Marie, she was sitting on a swing at the Wheatland city park. It was a nice, unusually calm, late spring day. The trees were budding with the good news that summer was on its way. The temperature was inviting enough for a light-sweater to keep you comfortable.

Marie was an attractive girl. Her Italian heritage was evident in her features and dark complexion. All three of their children were also dark complected, cute, and seemed well-behaved. Marie and Vangie met and began talking, so Milt

26

and I kept the kids occupied to allow Vangie and Marie to get to know one another.

Marie was vocal about not wanting to move to Wheatland. However, she wanted to give their new life in Wyoming a chance. Milt and I were pleased that Marie and Vangie seemed to hit it off. We were already good friends because of our relationship at the plant.

Working straight dayshifts at the plant allowed for much socializing that would be impossible once we were all on shift. We began having frequent picnics and spontaneous shared meals with the Marquettes during our tenure in Wheatland. Marie was an excellent cook and loved making Italian food. We certainly enjoyed eating it. We only knew Marie for a short period of time when she wanted to know if we would go "church hunting" with her and Milton.

I did not understand what all the fuss was about in finding a new Church. Don't get me wrong, I was still completely in awe at what happened at the river pumphouse at Four Corners along with my complete deliverance from alcohol through the temporary apple juice addiction. I just didn't know *what* we were supposed to look for in a Church. Therefore, we agreed to look for a church with them.

The first Church we visited together was The Church at Wheatland. Like many Churches in Wheatland, it was a small congregation. The small brown building with a faux steeple was next to Black Mountain Village, where we all lived. The Pastor was a construction worker at the plant and a weekend Pastor. His sermon was from the New Testament book of James. He seemed like a decent preacher to me. We sang a few hymns, and Church was over. I liked it. I was a bit taken aback when Milt and Marie soundly nixed it. They said we would keep looking. I knew they were looking for a non-denominational Church if possible.

The next Sunday was Wheatland Bible Church. Gordon Swenson was the Pastor. He was a small, aging, lighthearted man who resembled a happy little garden gnome. You could tell he thoroughly enjoyed preaching. The music service was far livelier than either the Christian Church or the Church at Wheatland. I was pleased and knew this was the one… *Nope.* As it turned out, it wasn't the one, at least not for Milton and Marie. Vangie and I continued to attend for several weeks because I liked Wheatland Bible Church.

About 4 weeks later, Milton and Marie found a Church they liked much better than Wheatland Bible Church. They said it was a "new work here in Wheatland." The Pastor was a man named Chan Bayne. They were holding services at the old Parks and Recreation Building. It was a tiny, cinderblock box-like building they rented for a couple of hours each Sunday morning. The Church was called Alliance Faith Chapel. We agreed to go there with them.

The first Sunday we went to Alliance Faith Chapel, I was shocked to see how few people were there. Most of the Church congregations in Wheatland were small. Wheatland Bible Church probably had 100 people, and it was one of the larger, if not the largest congregation in town. When you are in a small town that has dozens of Churches, the congregations divide out and tend to be quite small.

There wasn't a piano or organ at Alliance Faith Chapel, but a tall, lean construction worker named Mel Bindas, wearing oversized horn-rim glasses and sporting extremely thick, curly hair, played guitar and led the worship service. *It was the most amazing worship service I ever attended.* I could not believe there weren't more than 20 or so people in that building. It was as if the heavens opened, and choirs of angels were singing with us. I had never experienced anything so wonderful, and I did not want the worship service to end... *Ever.*

After Mel finished leading us in worship, Chan Bayne delivered the message. He was a gaunt man and appeared to be in his early 40's with a smile that would engulf his entire face, much like a caricature. Chan's message that day was deep but excellent.

Most messages I heard in my limited Church life were centered around Christ and His gift of Salvation to mankind. Chan's message that morning was much deeper spiritually. I was intrigued.

The service closed with a few more worship songs. I now understood more of what Milt and Marie sought in a Church. You could literally feel the presence of an Almighty God there. Frankly, it was the first time I was excited about returning to a Church. A new door opened. A door to a place of peace, wonderment, and the presence of God that transcended what was previously simple, blind faith.

As the summer slowly faded, the inevitable day came to start shift work. Energizing the in-plant electrical busses (the term for the in-plant switchgear and circuit breakers) was the first major step to testing plant equipment and filling/flushing water systems. I was overjoyed that the plant was slowly coming to life, but my stress was building with the realization that the heavenly dayshifts were coming to an end. I was not looking forward to going back to shift work. I was also thinking a lot about the Church. *Every week, I looked forward to returning to Alliance Faith Chapel for the amazing worship and fellowship.*

I volunteered to teach the new, locally hired operator trainees to thwart some shift work. I wasn't necessarily good in the classroom, but the alternative was to go on shiftwork right away. It was a difficult choice, but no one else seemed particularly interested in the teaching gig, and it meant a month or more of dayshifts. I couldn't ignore this.

In addition to Vangie's progressing pregnancy, we experienced another big event. We bought a house. In 1979, mortgage interest rates were about 14% or more. It made home ownership a very challenging quest for younger couples. However, the Wyoming Community Development Fund (WCDF) offered a limited number of 7% interest rate mortgages. There were many rules and regulations to qualify for these mortgages, but it was a jackpot if you qualified!

One of the rules was you must have a minimum of $1,200.00 in savings that could be used entirely to purchase the new house. It was simply down-payment money. This was money we didn't have. $1,200.00 in 1979 was a lot of free cash.

It took me three days to muster up the courage to call and ask Dad for a loan. I told him what it was for and that I would absolutely pay him back.

He thought about it for a minute and simply said, "It isn't a loan. I am sending you what should have been college money." It shocked me. There was no drama, no fanfare, no haranguing. He immediately followed through, and we received a check about 5 days later in the mail. I still think about this. His disappointment with my not attending college was extreme. However, it appeared he was getting over it.

We purchased a building lot with a nice, new modular home at 955 Elm Street in Wheatland. It was on a cul-de-sack. The builder/developer met all the requirements necessary to receive the WCDF funds. The house had three bedrooms and a full, unfinished basement with a single-car garage and a large dirt and rock yard. We would have to do the landscaping ourselves. No problem. We put in the lawn at our new house in Montrose a few years earlier.

Milt, Marie, Lorenzo Rodriguez and his wife Jen helped us move from the trailer house to our new abode. It was the only "fun" move we ever made. The men packed and moved the furniture and heavy stuff. Vangie, Marie, and Jen made lunch and dinner, helped unpack boxes, and arranged rooms. Lunch and Dinner was excellent, and it was the quickest, most efficient move imaginable.

In a single day, we were virtually settled in our new house. Obviously, there was a lot more to do, but the hard work of our friends was appreciated more than words could express. Some friendships we established during the early days of Laramie River Station endured a lifetime.

Autumn 1979 came upon us abruptly, along with the cold nights and the ever-present wind. Vangie and I were at Church one very chilly Sunday morning. There was no mistaking that Vangie was quite pregnant. She was not a big girl, which made her stomach look even larger. She was miserable most of the time but never complained. She, by nature, was not one to complain about anything, especially her health.

We had just finished an amazing worship service when Chan made a "special" announcement. He walked down the aisle and pointed to a young, rough-looking couple sitting right behind us. They were about our age, and she was holding a tiny baby.

Chan teared up as he extended his arm towards the small family. "We have a couple here living in their car right now while they look for work. Would anyone be willing to help them for a few days during this time of need?"

I looked back, and all I could see was that beautiful, helpless little baby in her arms. It was nasty cold outside, and I could not fathom a precious, vulnerable child being subject to the ruthless Wyoming weather living in a car. I didn't even ask Vangie her opinion. As usual, I leaped without looking. With a large, unfinished basement that was certainly much warmer than their car, we could put a bed and crib down there.

"We can help!" I quickly exclaimed.

Vangie looked at me like I was completely crazy. I never considered for the slightest moment that I was asking unknown people that I knew nothing about into our house when my wife was ready to burst with a child.

Their names were Pete and Fawn Albertson. Hmmm.... *Turned out the baby wasn't theirs. Fawn was just holding it.* Probably should have gotten a bit more information before thoughtlessly leaping into this. Pete and Fawn were trainwrecks on the same track. After Church let-out, we bought them lunch. Neither of them appeared to be wasting away. In fact, a few missed meals probably would have been a healthy alternative for them.

After arriving at our new home, they ambled right in, inspecting everything and proclaimed that it would do quite nicely. They asked to use the phone after **casing the joint...** Oops. Excuse me, that wasn't the right thing to say... After looking at EVERYTHING very, very carefully.

Why did they need to use the phone? They needed to call family members and tell them to "bring all their stuff to 955 Elm Street in Wheatland." The next day, a motley-looking bunch of people dropped a ton of stuff, including some furniture, right in our driveway blocking the garage door. Yup... We didn't just get Pete and Fawn; we also got their household possessions.

What a good husband I was. I was bringing people of unknown character, and murky backgrounds into my house with my 3-year-old daughter and excruciatingly pregnant wife. I mean, come on... *Just how thoughtful could a husband be???*

Vangie and I had a long talk that night. Okay, Vangie talked, and I listened. The wholly unkempt Pete would not be allowed in the house when I was not there. Period. It didn't matter how awkward it was, I was going to make sure that when I walked out the front door, Pete was with me, and the door was locked behind us. She was utterly correct about everything she said that night, including me "losing my head" after one look at the baby in Fawn's arms.

Pete and Fawn were with us for a couple of weeks. Pete was unable to find a job in a town that was beckoning, even begging, people from all over the state and the rest of the country to come and help build this massive powerplant.

Even if Pete couldn't get hired as a laborer at the plant like he wanted, he probably could have become a cook at Vimbos', Taco Johns, Pizza Hut, or worked at one of the filling stations. Nope. He would not do any of these. He insisted that he should have a position at the power plant. While I always had a singular obsession with working at a power plant myself, I was willing to do ANYTHING to get a laborer's job. I'm certain Pete was not hired anywhere because he was holding out for a management position.

If things were not bad enough, just a few days after arriving, they became more demanding on access to the house and what groceries we should buy. It was beginning to get scary. Vangie succinctly broke down the situation using no uncertain words: I either got rid of them, or she (and Brandi) were leaving back to Montrose to live with her parents until our baby was born and Pete and Fawn were gone. *There was not a third option.*

I didn't blame her and certainly was not fighting her on it. It was just a tough thing to do at the time. I look back on it, and I probably should have called the police and had them escorted out of the house.

I decided to call in a favor. Remember Bob Mendara? He was the gas well-logger in Rock Springs who would someday be rich. Turns out that rascal actually made it!

We kept loosely in touch since Rock Springs, and that scoundrel apparently saved every paycheck he ever received and bought into an oil well logging company in Casper,

Wyoming, just as he said he would. He claimed it was growing by leaps and bounds, and he was a multi-millionaire. Who would have ever guessed? Not me, that's for certain.

I called Bob, told him I needed a favor while jokingly reminding him that he owed me. I told him about Pete and told him he needed a laborer job if he could get it. Bob never hesitated. He told me the power plant was "constantly sucking away his unskilled workforce," and he would gladly give Pete a chance. All I needed to do was get him to his facilities in Casper. As far as I was concerned, this more than made up for the work I did on his car and pickup in Rock Springs.

I then called Milt, asking to borrow his old blue Ford van for the afternoon. I explained the situation to him. From the very moment I volunteered to take in Pete and Fawn, Milt was concerned and not comfortable with them coming to our house. He was glad to let me use his van and would even accompany me in case things got "dicey." Milt was like a big brother to me.

Pete and Fawn were not happy about being forced to go to Casper with their belongings. Milt came over and was with me when I sprung on them that I secured a job for Pete in Casper, and we were taking them there immediately. I was ecstatic and thankful to have Milt's support during this situation.

We loaded their possessions in Milt's van and drove them to Casper, locating Bob's offices. The facility was large and impressive. Bob did well as he said he would. There was no one there because we arrived at about 8:00 in the evening, but we showed Pete where he must go in the morning to start work. We then rented them a hotel room near the office and gave them a little cash for food and a taxi.

Pete and Fawn were not at all happy about this. They made it clear they liked Wheatland and the accommodation we provided. Pete reminded me that he would have eventually procured a job and that I was just being terribly impatient. The problem is, I could never prove that he even looked for work during the weeks they lived with us. He would disappear each day until I got back from the plant. He said he put in applications, but I honestly don't know if he did or not.

Milt was the one who really surprised me that night. I was soft-peddling the situation as usual and trying my best to placate Pete and Fawn's concerns. However, when they started complaining about leaving them in Casper, Milt immediately became quite intense with them.

"Look..." he said bluntly from the driver's seat. "This is not up for debate. You have two choices here in Casper. The side of the road or the hotel. I don't care which one you pick." As awkward as it was, it did the trick. Pete and Fawn clammed up, eventually walking into the hotel without a word or a thank you. We unloaded their stuff into the room and what didn't fit sat in front of the hotel.

Milt and I talked incessantly as we drove back to Wheatland from Casper. I liked him more and more as time passed. Pete and Fawn? They never showed up at Bob's offices for the job. I talked to Bob the next afternoon. He never saw hide nor hair of them. I certainly learned a big lesson. Thank God that Milt was there to help me out with this situation.

Shortly after this incident, my training gig finished, and I was forced to resume shift work. There was no choice because unit – 1 was about the same condition as Vangie. She was about to give birth to our little boy, and the plant was getting very close to giving birth to its first batch of electricity.

I didn't mind shift work as much as I thought I would, mainly because there were so many interesting things happening at the plant. Joe Johnson was right. One new unit start-up is truly worth 10 years of experience. My learning curve was vertical. Plus, it was nice doing what I liked without the baggage of previous mistakes I made at Four Corners. *For the very first time in my life, I felt good about myself.*

CHAPTER 4
A NEW BABY AND A GAME CHANGER

Ultrasound technology was widely used by 1979. However, we didn't take advantage of it. I was convinced she was carrying a little boy. Maybe it was because we lost the baby in Rock Springs or already had a beautiful little girl. I don't know why I thought this, but I was certain it would be a boy. Again, we were going to name him Joshua David.

Vangie went into labor at about 5:30 in the morning on October 22, 1979. We quickly dropped Brandi off at Milt and Marie's and then went straight to Platte County Memorial Hospital in Wheatland. It was a small, older facility, but Doctor Gold, one of two doctors in Wheatland, was a younger man and seemed to be a decent physician.

About thirty minutes before Vangie gave birth, something came over me. It was panic of sorts. Something in my brain clicked, and all I knew was the baby had to be a *GIRL*. This did not make any sense whatsoever: none, zero, nada.

I banked on this baby being a boy for nine months of pregnancy. I didn't even consider any alternative. Yet, in the final 30 minutes, I was freaking out that it wouldn't be a girl. It absolutely had to be a girl. I didn't even know what to do if it weren't a girl. No matter how stupid or weird this sounds, this really happened.

Our little GIRL was born at approximately 7:30 on Monday morning, October 22nd, 1979. I was so relieved, and it made no sense. But it was good. I was happy. We decided to have Dr. Gold tie Vangie's tubes because we were stopping at two kids. He assured us there would be no lasting issues with tying her tubes. Unfortunately, she endured a lifetime of problems after the procedure. In retrospect, I should have received a vasectomy. Our Joshua David was going to come, *but not this way.*

Vangie and I did not even discuss girl's names, and now we must come up with one. Chan Bayne's next to the oldest daughter was named Britnee, and we liked the name. We decided we would call this feisty little girl Brittanie. Vangie chose the spelling. I didn't care how we spelled it; I just liked the name. Thank God our new baby, Brittanie, was beautiful and healthy.

A new home, a new baby, and a new powerplant. Honestly, what more could you ever ask? How about the once-in-a-hundred-year snow event? The winter of 1979 turned out to be one for the record books in southeast Wyoming.

It began snowing hard on a Wednesday and didn't stop for two full days. The Wyoming wind helped move the snow to the most inconvenient places. Our car was in the driveway, but you couldn't see it was even there. The snow drifted up to the eaves of the house. The plant used the huge coal-yard and heavy equipment to move snow and help clear the roads to town so workers could do shift relief. Even then, one of the crew's had to work multiple shifts due to no access to the plant.

It was the only time I ever walked into a large grocery store with empty shelves. They were stripped bare. It was very surreal to enter the Wheatland Safeway store and see the entire store stripped almost completely clean. The snowstorm prevented any trucks from restocking for several days. It was an eye-opening experience. Up to that time in my life, I always took for granted going to a grocery store and finding life's essentials. Thankfully, we had enough groceries to carry us. Plus, Milt and Marie helped with milk and a few other commodities.

A few weeks after Brittanie's birth, I went to Church without Vangie or the girls. Vangie was tired and Brandi had a cold. It was a good service, but nothing out of the ordinary. As usual, Mel Bindas artfully led worship, and the entire congregation was caught up in the beautiful, heart-felt worship that lifted up and exalted Jesus and the Holy Spirit. However, about half-way through the service something began stirring within me.

I began to feel as if I were wrapped head to toe in a thick, heavy, warm quilt. The music and people's voices were muffled, and I entered an almost semi-conscience state. It was a state of peace and calm that I never encountered prior to this. I was experiencing an unexplained and seemingly unwarranted bliss.

Church ended, and people began filing out of the small building. I slowly did the same but in a complete daze. I got into the car, sat for a few minutes, and then started crying. I felt a presence unlike anything I ever experienced. As this presence increased, my sobbing increased. I was overshadowed by a power infinitely greater than anything I ever felt. The stronger I felt it, the more I sobbed. I was entirely overwhelmed, in total awe, and completely insignificant all at the same time.

My sobs turned into audible, gut-wrenching cries filled with non-words, seemingly incoherent noises coming from my lips. I was crying out, and words of no meaning flowed freely from my mouth. The ice-cold car felt comfortably warm and safe as I held my hands above the steering wheel and began worshiping the most-high God. This continued for what I guess was 30 minutes or more. To this day, I have no idea how long it lasted.

I think I finally slipped into a peaceful slumber. When I awakened, I noticed my eyes were swollen, and my face was red and blotchy. Yet, I felt complete peace without reservation. I sat for a few more minutes before starting the car and slowly driving home.

Arriving at the house and entering the kitchen, Vangie greeted me. She looked at me and, with alarm, said, "What happened to you?"

I smiled at her and simply said, "I'm not really sure." She stared at me until I quietly went to our bedroom and changed my clothes.

I knew two things for certain. First, I was being truthful. I had no idea what happened that morning. Second, just like the compulsion to drink apple juice in Farmington, I felt compelled to read the Bible. I never really read much of it prior to this. I heard many sermons and read select scriptures, but I never sat and just read the Bible like you would read a good novel. For some reason I now had the desire. I also knew something else. I would never be the same again. Whatever happened was much, much larger than could be put into words.

From that day forth, I could sense a presence that was continually there. I knew it was within me, and yet it felt exterior to me but somehow attached. It was like a homing beacon implanted in my forehead. It didn't hurt; it wasn't annoying, but it was there continuously. I thought it would wear-off after a short time. It didn't. It was continuous. Day, night, it didn't matter, it was always there. It was comforting and distinct all at the same time. It became a guiding light to me. Every thought, everything I said, and every action I made was filtered through this continuous beacon. My perpetual foul mouth became painful. I could not speak in the manner I had for years because every expletive set off an alarm.

My vulgar mouth melted away in a matter of a few short days. There is no earthly explanation for what happened from this point forward. You don't have to believe this happened. However, as certain as I breath, it is completely true.

Life dramatically changed for us. All the incidents and details moving forward in this memoir may be hard to believe, but they happened exactly as I explained them. Most of these things can be independently verified in one way or another. They are not made-up, embellished, exaggerated, or contrived in any fashion.

There is a saying that we have all heard at one time or another... *"You can't make this stuff up."* I can attest that the things that began happening in my life fall directly into this category. You can't make it up. From that day forth, everything changed in my life and the lives of many people around me.

Way back in 1956, the esteemed movie maker Cecil B. DeMille produced the most expensive movie ever made at that time. It was called *"The Ten Commandments."* It featured a young Charleton Heston as Moses. While there were plenty of theatrics, it was a very solid movie in terms of presenting the Biblical version of the Jews's Exodus from Egypt and the parting of the Red Sea. About an hour into the movie, there is a scene where Charleton Heston states, *"I do not know what power shapes my way, but my feet are set upon a road I must follow..."*

I can attest that during this time, I shared a similar feeling. I knew that the God of Abraham, Isaac, and Jacob... The God that gave His Son Jesus as an offering for the sin of man was doing something in my life. I didn't know what was coming, but it was life-changing based on what happened and what I felt that day.

Chapter 5
Initial Energy at LRS

The plant activities continued increasing by the day. I worked a substantial amount of overtime and liked the huge paychecks accompanying the long hours. Unlike my experience at Four Corners, I was fully comfortable with operating because *I finally knew enough to not be dangerous to myself and others while at the plant.* I still had an incredible amount to learn, but I knew it would come with additional experience at the plant. I began feeling some respect for my knowledge and did not walk with my head down as I did at Four Corners.

Bert Donovan paired the control room operators together for the unit – 1 start-up. This is because all the control room operators for both unit – 1, and unit – 2 were hired at the same time, and unit – 2 was still a year away. Plus, learning to operate a new plant efficiently required substantial trial and error and it helped having two people share the duties.

I was paired with Don Pillar. He and I didn't get along well because we were rivals. Don was substantially smarter and had a year or so more experience than I. He and Dave Hermann were considered the two most intelligent people on the plant site. They were very careful to memorize as much information (and trivia) as possible and effectively spout it when it counted the most.

Like most of the control room operators, we all wanted to be the first person to close the generator circuit breaker and put the unit online. There can only be one first-time for any new power plant.

After many delays, the long and anticipated day arrived to make initial energy finally arrived. Don and I were on the afternoon shift (3:00 to 11:00). Because we were more rivals than working partners, we split the operating duties. One of us worked the turbine generator and support systems, and the other worked the boiler and support systems. We would swap from the boiler to the turbine every shift and then back again on the next shift.

That afternoon, I was on the boiler side and Don was on the turbine side. The plan was for us to start the turbine prewarming process. This was a long and boring task essential to starting a large General Electric steam turbine generator. You were not allowed to roll a cold turbine because the heavy, thick casings and turbine rotors must be thoroughly preheated by slow pressurization to prevent them from forming cracks and causing serious damage.

Since Don was on the turbine that evening, he initiated turbine prewarming at about 7:00 PM. I maintained boiler pressure and monitored the auxiliary systems. The next shift took over at 11:00 PM and continued the rotor and shell warming. The day shift was supposed to do the initial turbine roll and synchronize it to the grid for the first time. Don and I were both bummed out about missing the roll and initial synchronization.

The next afternoon, we arrived in anticipation of a running unit, except the stack still had the lazy, black smoke from the oil guns rolling out of it. If the turbine was running, they would have swapped to coal and put the precipitator and scrubber in service. The stack would have been clean.

Shift change revealed that there were numerous electrical issues that day, and they were anticipating rolling the turbine during the afternoon shift. I was so excited I could barely stand it. It was my turn to be on the turbine. I was on the boiler the night before.

That evening, more people were packed into the control room than any of us had ever seen before. Every Manager in the plant and a few from Bismarck (Basin Electric headquarters) were there. It was standing room only. The turbine was prewarmed, and Don was ready to start a coal pulverizer to effectively fire coal for the first time.

At about 8:30, I initiated the roll. Because the first stage and crossover temperature were marginal, I rolled at a slow rate and then had about a two-hour hold at 3000 RPM. All of this was governed by SALI (G.E. Starting and Loading Instructions). SALI was a complex set of charts used to determine the roll time, holds, soaks, and the loading rate necessary to keep the turbine from overstressing due to thermal differentials.

At 3600 RPM, I applied the excitation to the generator. Excitation is the D.C. power source that turns the rotating field in the generator into a giant, high-powered electromagnet.

I was shaking from excitement but trying to play Mr. Cool. I was trying my best to act professionally when, in fact, there was so much adrenaline in my veins, I am lucky my head didn't explode and kill several people from fragmentation.

Don was noticeably grumpy because he was on the boiler that night. I could not even believe that I might be *THE ONE* to initially synchronize Laramie River Station unit # 1 to the grid. I was praying under my breath that nothing would stop us from coming online and that I didn't screw-up something in the process.

The coveted moment finally arrived. This culminated over four years of construction activity and a half billion dollars (the total project was 1.5 billion in 1975 dollars). After applying excitation and adjusting the incoming voltage to match the system voltage, I inserted the large brass scope key and turned on the synch-scope. Bert Donovan was standing next to me and doing his best not to throw me out of the way and do it himself due to HIS excitement of the moment.

After adjusting the speed of the turbine, the synch scope was going dead slow in the fast (clockwise) direction. When the needle was a little before 12:00, I CLOSED THE GENERATOR CIRCUIT BREAKER. There was an ear-shattering **BLAM!** on the mezzanine deck. *The massive air-blast circuit breaker slammed closed as designed.* Bert yelled at Don to watch the steam drum level and then told me to apply some load to the generator.

Pressing buttons on the complex turbine control panel, I opened the control valves, and the large, red, digital MW meter slowly increased from 0 to about 30 MW. The drum level was going high, and Don yelled at me to slow down while he "caught" the drum.

It was glorious. It was like slapping a newborn baby in the butt and hearing it cry for the first time. Laramie River Station Unit – 1 was officially online, and I was the first person to *ever* synchronize it to the grid. I would later learn that no one except me cared about this unique statistic. It didn't matter. I will always cherish this event. Unit - 1 at LRS will always be *my unit.*

When shift change came that night, the control room cleared of the on-lookers. Bert was still there and a few of the front-office engineers, but things were almost quiet, and the unit was, surprisingly, still running. We let the next shift relieve us, and we went home. Though still excited about the events of the evening, I fell straight into bed and went immediately to sleep.

CHAPTER 6
THE NEW PLANT BLUES

Because the plant was new, it had its fair share of issues. One of our largest issues was the fact that unit – 1 was completed before all the necessary power lines into and out of the switchyard were completed. When Laramie River Unit – 1 came online, there was only one 230 KV transmission line in service.

Because this plant was uniquely on the interface between the nation's east and west power grid, there would eventually be several 230 KV and 345 KV power lines into and out of the plant switchyard. Unfortunately, this was not yet the case. With only one power line into the switchyard, we would experience a "black plant" each time this line tripped out for any reason.

When our only power line tripped and the generator was no longer producing power, there was no power to run anything in the plant. It goes dark. This is where the term "black plant" comes from. The plant literally loses all internal power, including internal lighting and goes dark. This is usually a terrifying situation, accompanied by water hammers, safeties blowing, and total chaos in the plant.

Water hammers would cause large steam and condensate lines to slam violently and shake the entire plant. It does not matter how big of a "he-man" you are; water hammers are unnerving. However, the turbine rupture disk rupturing was the pinnacle of unnerving events.

The condenser is under a very high vacuum. In fact, if the condenser's absolute pressure increases beyond 7" absolute (about 23" of vacuum), the turbine trips to protect the long, low-pressure blading from heating due to windage. Condensers are designed to operate under this high vacuum *but not positive pressure.*

The turbine exhaust steam stops flowing to the condenser when the turbine trips, but there are many other sources of steam still blasting into the condenser.

LRS Turbine Rupture Disks

When the condenser reaches about 5 psi of positive pressure, there are large, round, rupture disks on the low-pressure turbine that are made of lead. They will rip open and relieve the pressure in the low-pressure turbine and the main condenser. (See illustration above).

These rupture disks are up to 3' in diameter and are located on the main turbine low-pressure exhaust hoods. They are generally designed to vent this massive amount of steam

50

upwards. When the rupture disk(s) blow, it violently rips the heavy insulation from the turbine LP crossover pipe and spreads it all over the turbine deck and plant.

It resembles the sound that accompanies the lift-off of a large rocket. When the rupture disk(s) blow on a turbine, it is akin to an explosion, followed by the sound of a rocket launching. While we are only talking 5 or so psi, the size of the rupture disks and the amount of steam being vented is impressive and impressively frightening to experience first-hand.

We experienced numerous black plant situations in the first few months of plant operation. After each one, I would take note of what was done correctly and what things were problematic. I became proficient at handling black situations. So much so I became increasingly confident and comfortable with operating through these tense and stressful moments.

I had no idea during this learning period that my life would fundamentally change during a particular black plant situation I was soon to find myself in.

CHAPTER 7
THE RUPTURE DISK FAILURE

My entire life I always experienced vivid and highly captivating dreams. In fact, it is fair to say that my enjoyment of going to bed was connected to the nightly array of intense, surreal craziness we call dreams. Someone once asked me if my dreams were in color. They were in color and complete with smell, taste, and all physical senses. Dreams were a major and (usually) interesting part of my life. They had been since my youngest memories.

A few months after the initial start-up of unit - 1, I experienced a peculiar dream. I was sitting in the control room at the desk. I looked over my left shoulder at the generator portion of the control board, and there was 520 MW showing on the red digital meter.

As I looked at the generator area of the control board, an alarm came in above the panel. It was labeled *"Under Reactive Ampere Limit"*. This was called the URAL circuit. It told me that the excitation (the D.C. voltage to the rotating field in my generator) was too low. If not immediately corrected, the unit would trip. In the dream, I jumped up from the chair and ran to the control board. As I got to the control board, a second alarm located right next to the URAL alarm came in. It was *"Trip Timer Active."*

The G.E. Generex© excitation panel was black with two large meters and several rocker switches. It allowed me to put the generator voltage regulator from AUTO to MANUAL and manually control the generator voltage if necessary. In the dream, I did exactly as I was trained to do. I selected

MANUAL on the voltage regulator and laid on the increase button to increase the excitation and generator terminal voltage. As soon as I did this, the Maximum Excitation Limit alarm sounded, and a moment later, the unit tripped. Immediately after the unit tripped, an electrician named Gerry Shiftler came running into the control room with a horrified look.

"I forgot to tell you that I was working on the alarm circuits!" He blurted with terror in his voice. In the dream, I could sense his dread.

The problem here was simple. He was working on critical equipment and did not tell me. I reacted (properly) to the alarms, and the unit tripped. He was now facing disciplinary action, or possibly even termination for not following protocol and informing me what he was doing.

I immediately woke up from this extremely realistic dream. There was nothing surreal about it. I was unable to go back to sleep for a while because I was still "living" the dream, feeling like I just tripped the unit.

That morning, I awakened with the dream still fresh on my mind. I ate a bowl of cereal and went to work. I didn't tell Vangie about the dream even though it was still plaguing me.

Shift turnover that morning was routine. I was told about some minor issues from the night-shift operator, and that the unit was at full load. After accepting the shift, I did my readings for the logbook and reviewed the clearance log. However, I could not shake the dream from my mind. It was still incredibly vivid.

A couple of hours into the day, I was sitting at the control operator's desk and looked over at the generator portion of the control board. I did this several times because of the dream. This time was different. This time, just as I looked up, an alarm flashed and sounded. It was *"Under Reactive Ampere Limit"*. I went completely numb. After realizing this was real and not a dream, I jumped up from the chair and ran over to the generator portion of the control board. The second alarm came in as soon as I got to the board. It was *"Trip Timer Active."* I knew I only had a few seconds to do something before the unit tripped. Rather than responding properly and immediately increasing the generator voltage, I froze in complete dread, numb from the overwhelming memory of the dream just hours earlier.

Unlike the dream, I looked at the Generex Panel, and the voltages appeared okay. I remained mortified, not knowing what to do. After what seemed like an eternity, a razzed-looking electrician named Gerry Shiftler came running into the control room.

"Don't do anything! Don't do anything! I am working on the alarm circuits for the Generex system. I forgot to tell you!" He was out of breath and looked frantically at the control board.

I looked back at him and said, "You are lucky I didn't dump this unit!"

"I will be right back!" He exclaimed and ran back out of the control room. A few minutes later, the two alarms on the annunciator panel that I was responding to went out. Gerry came back into the control room. He looked stressed out, and his face was pasty white.

"I don't know what I was thinking!" He began to shake his head. "I was doing a work order to ensure the annunciator panel was connected to the proper outputs from the Generex system and forgot to tell you I would be testing the alarms. *It is a good thing you didn't do anything*!"

"I was about this close," I responded, holding up my right thumb and forefinger together. You won't believe why I didn't do anything."

I quickly told him about the dream. He looked at me incredulously for a moment, and then his countenance changed. He stared at me for a moment longer and then said, "I believe you." We talked for a few more minutes, and he thanked me profusely and left the control room.

This, in itself, was quite amazing. However, the rest of the story is mind-boggling (but true). Remember the earlier discussion on black plants? A few weeks after this incident, I was at full load on unit − 1, and the 230 KV line tripped, tripping my unit, and we went black-plant.

A plant mechanic/insulator named Reid Harrison was replacing lagging (insulation) on the turbine crossover pipe using scaffolding that he erected to do the job. Why was he replacing the lagging? Because a previous black-plant situation a few weeks earlier blew the rupture disk and severely damaged the insulation on the crossover pipe.

As soon as the unit tripped and the lights on the turbine deck went out, he descended the scaffolding. After safely reaching the floor and walking away from the turbine, the rupture disks blew, pummeling him with debris. A heavy block of calcium silicate insulation nailed him in the back of the head. He went down hard on the turbine deck and stopped breathing due to a very serious closed head injury.

At the very same moment Reid went down an electrician named **Gerry Shiftler** came up the west stairs onto the turbine deck and saw him hit the deck. Gerry was trained as an EMT and immediately performed CPR on Reid, *saving his life.*

Reid spent time in the hospital being treated for a closed head injury, eventually making a full recovery. I always wonder if he would have survived if Gerry Shiftler had not been there. First and foremost, plant personnel always avoided the turbine deck during any kind of trip, especially a black-plant trip. Secondly, the timing of Gerry's venture onto the turbine deck was perfect.

If Gerry had been terminated over his failure to alert me that he was working on the generator alarms that day... I can't help but think of the movie, *"It's a Wonderful Life,"* produced in the late 1940s with Jimmy Stewart staring as George Bailey... We do not fully see or understand this puzzle we call life. Every piece must fit together perfectly and be interlocked for the other pieces to fit properly.

Thank God I experienced that dream and the puzzle pieces fit together as they did. Reid Harrison was given a gift of life from a convoluted and complex set of circumstances. I still get chills thinking about how this entire situation transpired.

CHAPTER 8
THE DEATH OF LARRY

Not long after the dream about Gerry Shiftler, I experienced another chilling and perplexing dream. This time, it was about my brother Larry. It was a two-fold dream. In the first part of the dream, I saw myself going to work the next day as I normally did. As I walked into the control room for shift change, Bert Donovan and the control room operator I was relieving were there. For a reason I was unaware of, Bert spoke angrily to the control room operator.

In the dream, I walked over to look at the control board while he finished the butt-chewing he was giving the operator. Obviously, I didn't want to get involved with one of Bert's butt-chewings in any way. Bert had a volatile temper, and all the operators learned to be careful around him.

He then finished talking to the operator, turned, looked directly at me, and asked how my day was going. I told him it was okay. He then smiled at me, patted me on the shoulder, and left the control room.

There was nothing remarkable about this dream, but it was very detailed, clear, and distinct. This dream played out exactly the next morning as I saw it the night before. I could hardly believe it. Every little detail was identical, just as it was in the dream, including Bert patting me on the shoulder. This leads me to the second dream from that night.

Immediately after the "Bert" dream, I saw my brother Larry. It was a bit more surreal as many dreams tend to be. I saw him and his hot-rod Chevy pickup he was rebuilding. It appeared to be at our house in Wheatland, which was odd because he had never been there before.

I was telling him about Jesus in the dream. The dreamscape changed again, and I saw him at his house in Montrose, Colorado. I was there, and I was telling him about Jesus again. I then saw him with a profound and deeply sad face, with a huge gash on his forehead.

I was overcome with anguish at that moment. The next thing I saw was a coffin sitting at the Valley Funeral Home in Montrose. I immediately awakened when I saw the coffin and was overcome with emotion. I could not even go back to sleep for over an hour. Getting out of bed, I cried and prayed. I was asking the Lord what I was seeing. Eventually, I went back to bed and fell asleep peacefully until the alarm went off to start the day.

The dream was at the forefront of my mind as I ate my breakfast. I decided to tell Vangie about it.

"I think I dreamed that Larry died." She looked at me for a moment.

"What a horrible dream to have." She touched my hand. "What happened?"

"I don't know. He had a gash on his forehead. The weird part of the dream was his coffin was at Valley Funeral Home in Montrose."

"Why is that weird?" She asked with a puzzled look on her face.

"We have known the Kinsey's forever. In fact, when Larry and Mel's son Christopher died, the Kinsey's did the funeral and buried him for free." I thought about it for a moment. "I am hoping it was just a weird dream and not something more." Deep in my heart, I felt it was something more... Way more.

Vangie knew the Kinsey's owned the Montrose Funeral Home across the street from my childhood home. I grew up playing with Kent Kinsey, who was my age. It didn't make any sense that if Larry died, someone other than Duane Kinsey and Montrose Funeral Home would handle his funeral. I comforted myself with this thought. The dream must be wrong, yet I felt the anguish of the dream deep into my core.

Larry and his wife Melody had three children. Shawn, the eldest, was born in 1973. Christopher was born June 4th, 1977, and died tragically of meningitis a little over a month later, on July 24th, 1977. Melody got pregnant again, and their youngest son, Joshua, was born in November of 1978.

Larry was a wild one in his teen years. Dad and he could not agree on much of anything, and Larry was incredibly rebellious. To this day, I believe it was because they were so much alike. Dad saw everything he hated about himself in Larry.

Larry's wife, Melody, was pregnant with Shawn when they married. Larry's overly amorous ways caused problems for him many times in his teens. The saddest, albeit hilarious, of his many sexual misadventures was when Dad was selling an Apache© Pop-top camping trailer when we lived on First Street in Montrose. It was a small camper that could sleep several people after it was opened with its canvas "wings" spread.

Dad was trying to sell the camper the way things were sold prior to the internet. You simply put an ad in the classified section of the local newspaper. In this case, it was the Montrose Daily Press. Not long after the ad hit the newspaper, a family up the street called and was anxious to see the camper. Dad told them to come anytime, but it would work well if they came right then because other people wanted to see it. They agreed and came right over.

Much to the surprise and chagrin of my folks and the visiting mother and father, they found Larry and their daughter IN THE CAMPER in an extremely compromising situation.

I honestly thought my dad was going to physically kill Larry that day. Many similar incidents like this created a deep rift between them. In case you're wondering, *the people didn't buy the camper.*

Larry's behavior significantly improved after he married Melody. He was hired by Colorado Ute Electric Association and started working at the Hayden Coal-Fired Power Plant in Hayden, Colorado. This company also owned the massive Coal-Fired Power Plant in Craig, Colorado, along with several hydroelectric plants, including the Ames Generating Station in Ophir, Colorado.

Larry worked at the Hayden Coal Plant as an operator. He also worked as Colorado Ute's hazardous diver. There weren't many calls for hazardous diving within the company, but Larry loved scuba diving and strived to get all the certifications he could get. While not very often, he occasionally used his diving skills in the cooling tower basins at the plant while checking for pump issues.

A few weeks after my dream about him, Larry called me. We usually spoke about once a month so his call wasn't a surprise. However, the reason for the call was somewhat of a shocker. He worked for several months on a 1968 short-bed Chevy pickup and just installed a new 350 engine in it and wanted to "break it in by taking a trip." While I was previously aware of his excitement to rebuild this truck, I was surprised he wanted to come to Wheatland.

Larry and Melody had never traveled to Rock Springs or Four Corners to see us but decided to make this trip. Wheatland was by far the farthest away from the other two places that they never visited. However, it was late spring, and the weather was, overall, decent for travel.

I would have been far more excited about this if it were not for my dream. In fact, deep in my heart, I was devastated. This couldn't be a coincidence. I was hoping it was, but I doubted it. If I hadn't experienced the dream about Gerry Shiftler, I probably would have still been excited about his visit.

Larry and Mel arrived in Wheatland as promised. We were always close, even though he was older than me by five years. After they arrived in Wheatland to visit, I drove him to the plant and gave him the grand tour. He was impressed with how large and how nice the plant was. I then showed him the town of Wheatland and Black Mountain Village, where we lived prior to buying our house.

We had just driven by 2157 West Basin, our old trailer house, when I decided the time was right to discuss what I knew was going to be a dicey subject. "Larry, do you ever think about God?" I could see the surprise on his face as he formed an answer.

He laughed awkwardly and said, "Yeah, I swear a lot using his name." This was typical Larry. He could be an enormous smart aleck.

"I'm being serious. Do you ever wonder how we got here?"

"Yeah... Pretty sure mom and dad had sex." We both busted out laughing. I left myself wide open on this one. He had a very dry sense of humor. It was obvious engaging him would be difficult.

"Larry, I am serious. You know there is a God, right?"

"I don't know." He looked wistfully out the passenger window for a moment before shaking his head and asking me, "Have you turned religious or something?"

"Larry, it only makes sense. In fact, it makes sense when nothing else does. The Bible says that we have all sinned and fallen short of God. In fact, Jesus himself said that if you call someone a fool, you have already committed murder in your heart, or if you look at a woman and lust for her, you have already committed adultery..." Before I could continue, he cut me off.

"Crap! I am hopeless then because I haven't just looked at a lot of women and lusted, I have followed up and known them in the biblical sense!" He started laughing, but it was an awkward and strained laugh as he tried to break the thick tension filling the car.

I continued, undaunted. "Jesus died to forgive us. That is the whole, complete point. We have all sinned, and our only chance at life beyond death is to simply and honestly ask for forgiveness and believe that His Blood paid for our sins."

"WOW!" He exclaimed. "You're serious about this shit, aren't you?"

"I am serious, and you should be also."

"When did this big move to religion happen in your life?"

I proceeded to tell him about my experience at the river pump house at Four Corners and how I immediately quit drinking because of the extreme cravings for apple juice. Unfortunately, it didn't have the effect I was hoping for. I then told him about the Gerry Shiftler dream. This appeared to reach him a bit more. By the time I finished telling him these things, we were back in front of our house.

"I gotta be honest with you, Mark. You have *really* surprised me with your turning to religion. I'll think it over, and we can talk about it later. Let's go in right now and see if the girls have dinner ready."

Before I could say anything else he quickly jumped out of the car and dashed into the house. We continued to have a nice visit, but the subject of God or anything existential never came up for the remainder of their time at our house. In fact, he avoided looking directly at me during the remainder of our time together. I felt like a real pariah. They returned to Montrose the next day.

Mount St. Helens tragically erupted on May 18th, 1980, rattling the country. It was about a week after Larry and Mel visited. It took a few days for the disintegrated remains of that mighty mountain to find its way to southeast Wyoming, but its arrival was apocalyptic and sobering. The sun tried desperately to pierce the massive ash cloud, only to bathe the landscape in a depressing, somber yellow hue.

Wheatland turned dark and gloomy for three days, with ash settling like a delicate layer of snow on the landscape. It was hard to imagine a mountain disintegrating in a matter of seconds. Over 50 people and thousands of animals died instantly during the eruption. It was an ominous indicator of how fast life, and our environment can change.

Regardless of what happened at Mount St. Helens, life seemed to continue normally at the power plant. I finished an exhausting set of graveyard shifts, my strength and patience fully spent from the continuous lack of sleep.

The only nice thing about shiftwork was the 'long change' between finishing the graveyard shift (12-8) and starting the afternoon shift (4-12). We would finish our last graveyard on Thursday morning and not return to work until Tuesday afternoon of the next week. It was like a mini vacation once a month. I had been working extensive overtime so I thought it would be nice to go back to Montrose and visit our parents and family. A visit to Larry and Mel's was, of course, on the agenda.

The visit to Montrose went well. Traveling with 3-year-old Brandi and 7-month-old Brittanie could be challenging at times, but overall, the trip progressed quickly. We stayed at Vangie's parent's house on East Main Street. The city of

Montrose was renamed East Main to East Locust Street, but to me, it will always be East Main Street.

Their house was comfortable and welcoming. Plus, we had an automatic babysitter as her parents loved being with the kids. It allowed us to get out, see old friends, and not worry about Brandi and Brittanie for a few hours. Vangie especially enjoyed the small moments of freedom.

During one of these times when Vangie's parents were watching the kids, we visited Larry and Melody. They lived in a nice home in English Gardens, one of the newer areas of town. He took me for a ride in his pick-up and demonstrated the latest performance improvements since they visited Wheatland. While riding with him, I worked up the courage to continue the discussion that started during their visit to Wheatland.

"Did you think about God since we talked last?" He just looked at me with an exasperated expression on his face.

"Not much." He then looked right at me. "It appears you have because you're wasting my time discussing it again." He was trying to be obnoxious and succeeding. Talking to him about this was very stressful. I was not a gifted debater and had virtually no experience proselytizing anyone, let alone family.

"Larry, what if I am right and you are wrong?"

"Guess I will get to see all my buddies in hell."

"No, I am serious about this. Honestly, why won't you consider any of what I am saying?" I apparently pushed him too hard. His temper flared.

"I don't know what to think. You have obviously figured everything out, and I am glad for you, but I'm not sure about any of it. Besides, every religion claims to have *THE* answer!" He turned a corner and stepped hard into the throttle, allowing the rear wheels on the pickup to break traction and squeal in defiance. "This truck screams!" He proclaimed triumphantly, trying to change the subject.

"Larry, if I am right and you are wrong, you lose everything. If I am wrong and you acknowledge that Jesus is real and that he died to forgive you and give you a way into His kingdom, you have lost NOTHING!" I over-emphasized nothing to make a point. I then continued since it seemed I had his attention.

"The way I see it, God must be incredibly smart. He is so much smarter than we could ever grasp. Think about a newborn baby... You could hold them next to the control boards at the plant so they could see the complexity, and all they would know is they are hungry and nothing else. The contrast between us and God is thousands and thousands of times greater than this. I don't have to worry about Buddhists or any other religion because *He proved He was real to me!*" I gulped in some air and continued undaunted. "I think the Bible makes amazing sense, and I think you need to commit because I don't believe for a moment that if there is an afterlife, you will be lounging with your buddies. At least with Christianity, you can be forgiven. It seems like this is where Christianity is so much different. We are ALL completely screwed up, and if you believe and ask for forgiveness, it is there."

His countenance grew angry as he said, "Maybe you should concentrate on someone else." He then took his eyes off the road and looked over at me again. "Wow! You really have plunged head-first into this shit, haven't you?"

I ignored him and continued. "Will you at least concede there is a God?" I realized I was pleading with him. I didn't want to plead with him. He didn't answer immediately but continued driving for another minute or so.

"Maybe I will. You stop preaching to me and let me think about it."

"You better think hard because the Bible says our life is like a vapor, here and gone. It is THAT quick. None of us know how much time we have." As I spoke, the dream was at the forefront of my mind, but I knew I couldn't tell him about it.

"Got it. We're done with this subject. I told you I WILL think about all of this." I could tell by his voice inflection that the subject, for now, was closed.

We enjoyed the remainder of our visit with everyone. It was always nice to come to Montrose and see family and friends. The trip back to Wheatland was also good. Summer was in full bloom, and the kids behaved well.

Returning to Wheatland was always bittersweet. It was home, but it meant that we would fall back into the day-to-day grind of shift work and occasional trips to Cheyenne or Fort Collins to maintain our sanity.

Shortly after returning to Wheatland, Vangie and I decided to use some accumulated vacation time and visit my oldest brother, Wylie and his wife, Patricia in Montana. Due to my absolute loathing of graveyard shifts, I requested vacation for the second and third week of August. This, of course, was my graveyard shift in August. We decided to drive to Butte, Montana, where Wylie and Pat lived.

Wylie was working at the experimental MHD (Magneto Hydro Dynamics) facility. He left the Colstrip Generating Station in Colstrip a couple of years earlier to work for this government-funded start-up in Butte. We never visited him or his wife Pat in Montana and decided this would be a good time to do so.

Vangie loaded our yellow Ford Fairmont station wagon to the hilt with every conceivable item possibly needed by a family of four taking an expedition to Antarctica or some other equally remote site on this terrestrial ball. The tires on the small yellow station wagon groaned in protest of the weight. However, in fairness to Vangie, we truly never lacked anything while traveling.

Late in the evening, the day before we left for Montana, Steve Keller, an operator on my shift, stopped by and gave me three cassette tapes that he packed with contemporary Christian music. He knew there was a cassette player in the Fairmont and that I liked Christian music. The cassette tapes had no markings on them whatsoever. Apparently, he just filled them full of different music from different artists. I threw them haphazardly into the car's glove box before we left.

We never listened to any cassette tapes on the way to Butte due to having a small baby, an active toddler, and being in a station wagon with egregious road noise. However, the trip to Butte went well.

We thoroughly enjoyed our visit with Wylie and Pat. Wylie, and I spent an afternoon riding motorcycles in the mountains near his house. We enjoyed a great time together. We even drove by Evel Knievel's home, hoping to catch a glimpse of the fearless motorcycle gladiator. I always enjoyed being with Wylie, and this visit did not disappoint.

After two very enjoyable days at Wylie and Pat's house, we headed into Idaho as we had motel reservations at a 'Days Inn' in Pocatello. Our plan was to spend the night there before driving to Salt Lake City to visit a big amusement park. When finished in Salt Lake City, we were to go onto Montrose for a few days before returning to Wheatland.

At this point in our vacation, I did all the driving, including today's safari from Butte, deep into Idaho. We were about 20 minutes out of Idaho Falls when, without warning, I became immersed in an intense feeling of dread. I became nauseous and abruptly pulled the car over to the side of the road.

"What's going on?" Vangie's voice was full of concern as the car rumbled off the pavement onto the rocky shoulder.

"I'm not sure…" My voice trailed off. "Something really bad just happened."

"What are you talking about?" Vangie leaned forward and looked over at my face with alarm.

"I don't know… I just don't know. Something just happened. I am sick to my stomach." I felt like I needed to throw up. Without saying another word, I got out of the car, walked to the roadside, leaned over, and put my hands on my legs above my knees. Brittanie woke up and started crying.

Vangie unstrapped her seatbelt, leaning over the front seat to tend to her.

A few minutes passed, and my nausea subsided. However, I was rattled to the core. I slowly got back into the driver's seat, sat for a minute, then turned to Vangie and said, "Let's just get a motel in Idaho Falls. It is only a few miles from here. I don't think I can go on to Pocatello."

Vangie was concerned and exasperated at the same time. "Don't we already have reservations in Pocatello?"

"Yes, but I don't think I am up to driving there." I was still reeling from the all-encompassing anxiety enveloping my being.

"What's happening with you? Do you need to go to the hospital?" Vangie was confused and frustrated as she probed my apparent incapacitation.

"No, I am fine. I can't explain it." I trailed off for a moment before continuing. "But I think Larry may have just died." There, I said it. No matter how nuts it sounded, I said it.

Vangie stared at me with puzzled eyes for a minute or so before pensively asking. *"Why would you ever think that?"*

"Vangie, I just know it. Don't ask me to explain because I can't." I looked into her eyes and tried to convey the depth of my foreboding. "Let's just get a motel in Idaho Falls."

She stared at me for a few more moments. "Let me drive from here. Move over and sit this out for a bit, and I will drive onto Pocatello." I took her advice, exiting the car and walking to the passenger side. She slid across the front and into the driver's seat. We eased back onto the road and headed south.

There were no cell phones in August of 1980. Luckily, Mom and Dad were aware of our itinerary and knew that we were staying in Pocatello that night. In the hour or so it took to get to the Days Inn in Pocatello, I calmed down but felt completely exhausted. Vangie pulled into the motel lobby area, and I got out of the car and went to the hotel's front desk to register.

Once at the front desk, I took out my credit card and said, "I'm Mark Gregg, and I have reservations here tonight." The desk clerk was a heavy-set woman in her early thirties. Her eyes widened as soon as I said my name, and she seemed to panic a bit.

"Mr. Gregg, you need to call your dad as soon as possible, there has…" She looked away for a moment and then back into my eyes. "Just call your dad as soon as possible. I have your room key right here. You can bring your credit card back when you are done." She handed me the room key. "You are on the bottom floor just around the corner." She quickly pointed to the right side of the lobby.

I knew then that Larry was dead. I walked out of the lobby in total shock, passing the car without saying a word to Vangie. I went to a pay phone in the portico by our room and made a collect call to Dad's house. He answered the call and quickly accepted the charges from the operator.

"Are you in Pocatello?" Dad asked solemnly.

"Yes, just arrived," I answered pensively. "What's going on?"

71

"Your brother Larry is dead." His voice was slow, strong, and matter-of-fact. I did not detect any emotion, certainly not the emotion of a man who just lost his 28-year-old son.

I was overcome with grief again. "What happened?" My voice cracked. I was trying unsuccessfully to not let emotion overcome me.

Dad continued talking as if it were a distant relative and not his son Larry. "We are still waiting for answers, but it sounds like he drowned." His voice lowered as he succinctly stated, "Apparently, he was doing a diving job at the Ames hydro station in Ophir, but something went wrong." I couldn't hold it back now and began to sob. Dad remained unwavering.

"Wylie and Pat are on their way from Butte. They want you to remain at the Days Inn and wait for them." He paused for a moment. "They can stay the night at your hotel, and then you both can drive here sensibly." His voice took on an air of anger. "I don't need to lose another son from a car wreck because either of you was too tired to stay awake."

I couldn't focus and was trying to speak without crying as I said, "I will call you when Wylie arrives. Maybe you will know more about what happened, then." I hung up the phone and went back to the car. As soon as Vangie saw me, she started crying. She knew before I said anything what I was about to tell her.

"Larry drowned a couple of hours ago." Tears were streaming down my face. I felt grief beyond any I had ever felt before. "Wylie and Pat are on their way here."

Vangie got out of the car and hugged me tight. We were both crying. Neither of us ever dealt with the death of

72

someone close. After a long, sobbing embrace, I parked the car and grabbed one of the suitcases. I took Brandi by the hand and walked slowly into the motel room.

"Why are you crying, Daddy?" Brandi asked as she started to cry softly. She had never seen her Daddy and Mommy get this upset before and it was obviously unsettling to her.

Vangie answered her before I could. "Daddy just got some bad news. He will be okay."

Vangie sat in the armchair in the corner of the room while holding Brittanie in her arms. I finished unloading the car and then fell face-first on the bed in grief. I was swimming in emotion, guilt, and confusion.

Should I have done more to talk to Larry? Should I have warned him about the dream? Did I do enough? My emotions and thoughts were muddled and perplexed.

After a few minutes there on the bed, I stood up and walked out of the room. Seeing the payphone in the portico, I decided to call Milton. I was probably as close to him as anyone besides Vangie. I felt compelled to talk to him. When I placed a collect call at his house, I was surprised when he answered the phone on the second ring.

"Milt, my brother Larry just died." I immediately felt a release as I spoke those words. Milt only Met Larry for a few minutes when he and Melody visited Wheatland 3 months earlier.

"I am so sorry, Mark." Milt seemed overcome with emotion. "I will pray for you and your family. Thank you so much for calling me."

"Thanks, Milt. I have to go now. I will let you know when I know more." I hung up the phone. This was the first of two very odd things that rescued me from my sorrow. I later learned that Milt was racked with grief and even missed work the next day. Yet, immediately after the call, I began feeling strangely at peace. The second thing that happened circulates often through my memory to this day.

I went to the car and sat in the driver's seat. I don't know why I did this as opposed to returning to the room to be with Vangie and the kids. I opened the glove box and saw the three cassette tapes Steve Keller gave me. They were nondescript, as he had packed them with Christian music and did not label any of them. *Randomly* grabbing one of them, I popped it into the cassette player. A song that still sends chills down my spine to this day immediately started at the beginning. It was called *"Water Grave"* and was recorded by a Christian band named "Dogwood."

The song started with an acoustic guitar solo followed by a low-key, somber male vocalist. The lyrics immediately caused the floodgates of my emotion to pour forth:

"In my house, there's been a mercy killing."

"The man I used to be has been crucified."

"The death of this man was a final way of revealing, in a spiritual way, that to live, I had to die."

"Now, if I let a dead man linger in me, I might get a little idle in my ways."

"So I am going down to the celebration river."

"Gonna take this dead man down to his water grave."

There is a refrain of drums and guitars, and the chorus vigorously breaks forth:

"I'm going down to the river, my Lord."

"I'm going to be buried alive."

"I want to show my heavenly Father that the man I used to be, has finally died."

The chorus repeats with additional vocalists.

It was as if the Lord God Almighty opened the heavens and spoke directly to me. How could Steve have known what was about to happen when he recorded numerous songs from different artists?

How could I randomly pick one of three unmarked cassette tapes haphazardly thrown into the glove box of our car, and this song, these words of death and redemption, freely flow forth from the cassette player? This was the first song to play when I inserted the cassette into the player. I did not have to hunt for it or listen to any other song. For those who do not believe, I am sorry. However, this is precisely how it happened.

My mom later told me that Larry was not his usual cocky self the night before going to the Ames Hydro plant in Ophir. She told me that Melody said he seemed concerned, even

75

worried about what needed to be done there. He apparently said something else that I will never forget. At some point during the evening, he casually mentioned to her, "Maybe Mark is right about God." I can't attest to this, but it is what my Mom told me at the funeral.

Larry was inside the penstock of the Ames hydro plant when he drowned. This is the pipe that directs the flow of water from an alpine lake into the hydro turbine. He was in about 3 or 4 feet of extremely turbulent water. Technically, it was not a scuba dive. He was not wearing scuba gear. He was wading when the turbulent water currents apparently overcame him.

There was a deep, nasty gash on his forehead (just like I saw in the dream), but the autopsy said the official cause of death was drowning. I will always believe that he accepted Christ as his Lord and Savior and then went to his water grave precisely as the song said.

After the call to Milton and the episode of Water Grave, I experienced a peace that passed all understanding. I spoke bluntly and purposely to all of Larry's friends, and was a bedrock of strength to my family and everyone else. I don't know if I "reached" any of Larry's friends with the message of Jesus Christ, but they were polite and captive audiences due to the somber circumstances.

The surprising and final confirmation of the dream was as compelling as the rest of the incidents surrounding Larry's death. Remember when I said that Larry's casket was in the Valley Funeral Home, not Montrose Funeral Home (Kinsey's)? If you recall, I used this very detail to help talk myself out of the dream being prophetic prior to his death.

Wouldn't you know? Kinsey's unexpectedly sold Montrose Funeral Home several weeks prior to Larry's death, and Duane and Edna Kinsey retired. For whatever reason, when Dad, Mom, and Melody looked for a funeral home to handle Larry's funeral, they chose Valley Funeral Home instead of what used to be Kinsey's Montrose Funeral Home.

When I walked into the room where Larry's "viewing" was held, His casket was sitting exactly as I saw it in the dream. I saw the room, the casket, and the very setting where his "viewing" was held. This was several months before his death.

Larry was the first family member to die in the Lewis F. Gregg household. It was difficult, but after the events described, I felt peace about it that no one else in the family had. Dad never showed much emotion before, during, or after the funeral. I think I have always held that against him in some odd way. However, it never came to the surface to anyone except Vangie. I told her on more than one occasion that Dad's lack of emotion surrounding Larry's death always bothered me.

The trip back to Wheatland was somber but quick. Upon arriving back to work I was barraged with well-wishers telling me how sorry they were. I appreciated their sentiments and heartfelt condolences. However, no one was as broken and sincere as Milton. After returning to Wheatland and hearing that he was wracked with grief after our phone call, I realized that intercessory burden-carrying was a real thing. I couldn't explain it, but I experienced it with Milt. We would always be as close as brothers after this.

CHAPTER 9
PROMOTION AND SELF-INFLICTED WOUNDS.

Employee turnover in plants the size of Laramie River Station was continuous. Especially when the plants were new. This was particularly true in the early 80's because they were building so many new coal-fired plants. It was usually quick and easy to find another powerhouse job when you were angry with your boss, or if your wife hated where you lived, or if you were just plain bored and wanted something different. Laramie River Station was no different.

Due to expected turnover, the original Shift Supervisors and Assistant Shift Supervisors began taking other in-house positions created in maintenance, maintenance planning, and other day-shift positions. Plus, some people received offers they could not refuse from other power plants. This took several people into different jobs by the time unit – 3 was operational.

The original Control Room Operators that started with me on February 12th, 1979, began moving to the Assistant Shift Supervisor position on a regular basis. The upward movement was largely by seniority/age. Ed Simpson was among the first to be promoted. He was good friends with Bert Donovan when they were together in North Dakota.

One by one, we were promoted to Assistant Shift Supervisor. Dave Hermann and Don Pillar went before me. It was then my turn. Milt came immediately after me. I was only 25 years old, and many of my crew members were older than me. Plus, I possessed the maturity of a 3rd grader and loved practical jokes. It's a very bad combination for a supervisor.

I was a decent control room operator but far too immature to be promoted to supervision. I often wondered why I left the control room operator so soon but realized if I stayed, people I felt were far less qualified than me would move up. It doesn't matter why I took the job; I was simply promoted too early. It almost ruined my career.

Shortly after our promotions, Milt and I ended up on shift with Mort Grannitelli, who almost immediately moved from Assistant Shift Supervisor to Shift Supervisor. He was very loyal to Bert Donovan, and Bert, being a good family man, never heard the rumors of Mort's issues with his current and former wives. Bert just knew that Mort would do anything for him. Bert liked this. Frankly, to this day, I think very highly of Bert and his knowledge of plant operations. Unfortunately, his biggest fault was desiring absolute allegiance. This caused him many issues at LRS.

As time passed, my issues with the Graveyard (night) shift intensified. By the time the final night shift arrived, I was so happy and relieved to be finishing this draconian horror of life deprivation that I would invariably find new and novel ways to cause issues for me and others. It became my personal hallmark, getting into trouble on my final night shift each month.

The first incident involved Mike Sciorra. He was a Boiler Attendant on our shift. The Boiler Attendant was the bottom or lowest-level operator in the plant. The only thing less than a Boiler Attendant was a laborer. The Boiler Attendants ran the bottom ash system, moving thousands of tons of ash out of the bottom of the furnace and into the ash ponds.

Boiler Attendants stayed in their own little "shack" on the bottom floor under the boiler. They would rest there after operating the ash system and doing their equipment checks.

This "shack" was an appropriate 12' x 12' well-lit, metal office with windows around the perimeter. In the case of Mike Sciorra, it would allow them to get out of the heat and noise of the bottom ash area and do their logbooks, study, or SLEEP.

Mike was so lazy that we often commented he would asphyxiate himself if breathing weren't involuntary. As a new, proud, young, undisciplined, and completely immature Assistant Shift Supervisor, I would hide behind beams until I saw him underperforming. This usually took less than a few minutes. I would then catch him in the act and ream him.

On one of our final night shifts (our last in a series), I called him to the Shift Supervisor's office and reamed him in front of several others because, during shift change, the previous shift complained about him always leaving a mess and not doing his job.

I ended this serenade with, "Mike, if you don't get out of the BA shack and do your job, I am going to blow your ass out of there!" *Hmmmm.... What does this even mean?* Blow you out of there? Immaturity and silliness are potential for a really bad situation. I gave an ultimatum and now must follow it up. True to my curse of really screwing-up on the final night shift, I went to the water lab and did the unthinkable.

The water used in a high-pressure steam plant is incredibly pure, and there is an entire staff of laboratory technicians who continuously test the water and manage the water treatment facilities. The laboratories in modern power plants are equipped with extensive high-dollar testing equipment and a lot of chemicals, reagents, and other 'labby' stuff.

If you put ammonia (NH3) over iodide crystals, you create Nitrogen Triiodide. Once the ammonia evaporates, the crystals are extremely unstable and will vigorously pop or snap, giving off a brownish-red smoke and staining anything it touches. It is a cheap, easy to concoct, contact explosive and not particularly dangerous unless combined in large quantities.

Later that morning before shift turnover with the dayshift, I went to the lab and made a small batch of Nitrogen Triiodide. I called and asked Mike to go check something in the plant. Once he exited the Boiler Attendant Shack, I spread some of the moist crystals on the chair in the BA shack. It is stable until it dries. Once it dries, the slightest touch will cause it to snap or pop.

Three or four of us were hiding behind I-beams waiting for Mike to return to the BA shack. Eventually he plodded laboriously back to the shack, pulled open the door, and dropped down in the chair. We could not see the lower part of his body through the windows. All we saw was him sitting down and then immediately jumping back up, accompanied by the whiff or puff of brownish colored smoke that occurs when the compound explodes. As anticlimactic as it was, I opened the door to the BA shack, laughing hard. It stunk like iodine in the shack. Mike looked really pissed.

"What the hell did you do?" He exclaimed angrily. I never saw this side of him before. I was worried for a moment he might try and punch me. Though slow and lazy, he was in great physical shape and not much older than me.

"Lighten up!" I retorted. "I told you I would blow your ass up if you didn't get out of the BA shack and do your job."

"Very fricking funny! I didn't think *anyone* could be so damn childish." He was *incredibly* angry. I was shocked at the intensity of his anger. In retrospect, I should have seen this coming. He was right. It was a highly stupid, childish thing to do. I left the BA shack and returned to the office still laughing about his reaction.

Shift change came and I was now free of night shifts for several more weeks. I was elated and giddy. After shift turn-over, I went home and went to bed. I always tried to get a bit of sleep after my last night shift, otherwise, I was just too groggy, grumpy, and miserable to be worth anything to anyone.

I was not in bed for more than a few minutes when Vangie came into the bedroom.

"Mark, wake-up." She shook my arm. "Are you awake?"

"What's wrong?" I turned and looked at her. "Is something wrong?"

"Dallas Wade is on the phone and says he needs to talk to you immediately." Dallas Wade was the Plant Manager. This was several levels up from me, which could not be good. I got out of bed and went to the phone. Dallas possessed an extremely deep, authoritative voice.

"Mark, Dallas Wade here. You need to come back to the plant right now. We have a serious issue." His voice was stern, his statement terse, and it scared me.

"I will be there shortly," I replied.

"Come straight to my office when you get here." He immediately hung up the phone.

"What's going on?" Vangie asked me with due concern.

"I think I may have really screwed up." I looked at her with abject fear in my eyes. "I played a stupid trick on Mike Sciorra, and I think he must have reported me."

She just shook her head and said, "You better get in there and straighten this out." Her eyes flashed with anger. We owned a house, had two young children, and had no savings. Getting fired would be a HUGE problem.

I quickly dressed and drove to the plant. Though shaking in my boots, I walked boldly into Dallas Wade's large office. Several people were there including Mike Sciorra and Jerry Johnson, a union steward. Mike was bent partially over with a pained look on his face. There was a towel wrapped around his slacks at waist level, hanging just above his knees.

Dallas looked at me and said, "Mark, we have a serious problem." His speech was slow and measured. "I want you to be truthful and tell me what happened this morning." Bert was also in the office, along with Gordon King, the operations supervisor, and another person I had never seen before.

I thought quickly and realized there was no use playing games with this. I told them word for word what I said and precisely what I did. I didn't waffle or make it sound less than it was.

They all listened until I was done. Dallas was the first to speak. "You took dangerous chemicals from the lab without authorization and used them to seriously burn Mike's buttocks, ruining his slacks." He paused and looked at me with fire in his eyes. "Do you see a problem here?"

"Yes, sir." My voice was shaking because I knew then I was getting fired. "I realize now that I didn't consider the consequences and screwed-up. I intended this as a joke. I never intended to burn or hurt Mike or damage anything. This is the honest truth."

Jerry, the Union Steward, spoke next. "It is the Union's position that he should be terminated for intentional negligence. We also urge Mike to get an attorney and file charges against Basin Electric and Mark." I felt light-headed and nauseous for a moment. Not only was I getting fired, *I was probably getting sued.* This whole thing was moving far beyond just getting fired.

Bert immediately took the floor. Bert was the oldest person in the room and carried a reputation as a total hard ass. I didn't know if I could stand him railing on me right now. If they were going to fire me, they just needed to do it. I now fully understood the gravity of the situation and just wanted the inquisition to end.

Bert looked at Mike and the union steward with acrimony in his eyes. "How many of you, including Mike Sciorra or you, Jerry, have ever been involved in any horseplay?" Bert's demeanor was extremely condescending. "Honestly, have any of you ever been involved with horseplay or *am I in the presence of angels?"*

Dallas retorted. "Bert, this is more than horseplay."

"No, it really isn't." His eyes narrowed, and his voice lowered an octave as he growled, ***"Let him among you who is without sin throw the first stone."*** Bert's irate stare was bearing down on both Jerry and Mike. He then looked at me with total irritation in his eyes and asked, "Mark, tell me the truth. Have you learned a damn lesson here?"

I was still reeling over his *"...throw the first stone"* remark. I honestly couldn't believe he just said this. Judging by the looks on their faces, I don't think Dallas or anyone else could believe it either. It was truly a surreal moment that I have replayed in my mind hundreds of times.

"Absolutely," I answered, slowly shaking my head. "Frankly, I feel like an idiot and unsure what possessed me to do this." Fortunately, my shame and repentance were sincere.

Bert then raised his arm and pointed in the direction of his office. "Go to my office and wait for me there." The entire scene reminded me of when I was a kid when Mom or Dad would do the same thing.

Before leaving, I looked at Mike Sciorra and said, "Mike, I honestly apologize. I did a stupid thing without thinking it through. I hope you will forgive me for being an idiot." I then turned and walked into the hall slowly down to Bert's office.

Time slowed to a crawl. My stomach hurt, and I was terrified. I could not even imagine how I would tell Vangie I was fired, and worse, I could not imagine how we would live. We didn't have a penny's worth of savings. We were living paycheck to paycheck. This was bad. Real bad.

It seemed like years before Bert walked into his office. He looked pissed when he finally arrived.

"I hope you learned a damn lesson. I just groveled to keep you from getting fired." I immediately felt 100 tons of weight lift off me. I didn't know what to say.

"Here's the deal." He looked at me with an icy stare and continued. "You're getting five days off without pay. You are going to buy that asshole Sciorra, slacks, and underwear, and you will NEVER pull a stunt like this again." He paused and lowered his voice. "Do you hear and understand me?"

I felt like the heavens opened and choirs of angels sang as I gushed, "Yes, sir, I FULLY understand. You cannot imagine how thankful I am to you for what you said and did for me in there." My emotions were almost overwhelming me.

"You should be. What you did was ridiculously stupid. Next time, use your head. You are a smart guy, start acting like it."

We talked a few minutes longer. He told me not to come in for my first five afternoon shifts the next week. I thanked him several more times before going back home. Facing Vangie was much easier now than if I was fired. She was still seriously miffed at me, but at least I was still employed.

I was supposed to have my long change and then five more days off without pay. However, on Monday of the next week Bert called and said they were seriously short-handed and just to come in, work my afternoon shifts, and keep my mouth shut. I worked the entire week and there was never a penny taken from my paycheck nor another word said to me about this incident. ***Thank You, Jesus.***

Did I learn my lesson? No. Unfortunately, being childish and immature does not pass overnight. My next faux paus was equally stupid but got me a misplaced "attaboy."

Due to the employee turnover discussed earlier, we were constantly training new Control Room Operators. One of these trainees was Gary Kellogg. Gary came from a small plant in Minnesota. He sported massively thick, mutton chop sideburns and a slight, rather amusing, speech impediment. Okay, maybe not an impediment. It was more of a northern accent combined with an odd, halting mannerism. He was also prone to inventing new words that he used indiscriminately.

Gary worked as a floor operator at LRS before being promoted. Management was initially reticent to promote him, but he was a hard worker and did a mediocre job on his promotion testing. Turnover reached the point where Gary was far better than the alternatives, so he was moved up to the control room.

He was put on my shift to work with an experienced Control Room Operator, Keith Holman. Keith was a few years older than me and came from an old cogeneration facility in Cedar Rapids, Iowa. He was a prickly, occasionally outright offensive person but highly confident of his abilities. However, what I considered his "minimal" abilities" probably saved my job. I will always be thankful to him. His hands were full while training Gary Kellogg.

Gary was a chain smoker and extremely skittish. Being promoted to Control Room Operator put tremendous stress on him. He paced up and down the control board like a caged animal, smoking continuously. Every time an alarm sounded, he instantly cranked his neck and head to find the offending panel alarm and then sprinted to the control board area to see what was happening. After many days of training with Keith, he was still wound tight as a drum.

I talked to him several times, telling him to relax. I tried to convince him that his tension and over-reaction would work against him when something major happened. He always thanked me and promised to try harder, only to immediately resume the caged-animal pace in front of the board.

On our last graveyard shift, I was, once again, feeling giddy about finishing nights. I decided to 'help' Gary calm down a bit. I pulled Keith Holman into the Shift Supervisor's office.

"Keith," I said, looking out at Gary pacing the board." I am testing 'A' Boiler Feed Pump turbine's overspeed trip. It will bring in the alarms like it has tripped, but I will have it locked out. Don't let Gary do anything stupid."

"You sure you should be doing this?" Keith asked apprehensively.

"It's fine. Don't worry about it. Just make sure Gary doesn't overreact and screw something up."

Keith replied, "Okay, if you say so," in an irritating, patronizing voice as he shrugged his shoulders and walked back into the control room, shaking his head. I felt he was over-reacting to the situation.

LRS has three boiler feed pumps on each unit. Two of them are 12,500 horsepower steam turbines that spin at almost 6000 RPM. The other is an electric start-up pump that uses a huge, 6,000-horsepower electric motor. The start-up pump was used during start-ups or if one of the steam-driven units was out of service. Obviously, it could only pump about 50% of one of the steam turbine units but could still carry a fair amount of load on the unit.

The steam turbines are equipped with sophisticated overspeed prevention devices. If the coupling between the pump and turbine broke, or if the pump went dry, the turbine speed would instantly accelerate due to the load loss and turn the turbine into a huge grenade. The overspeed protection device was designed to abate the speed increase by instantly slamming the steam inlet valves closed.

An established procedure was to test the overspeed prevention circuit without tripping the turbine. When you did so, it would activate the overspeed trip alarms in the control room but would not actually trip the turbine and pump. I would exercise the overspeed circuit, activating the alarms in the control room, making Gary think the turbine tripped.

I went down to the two large, screaming boiler feed pump turbines. The unit was at about 550 megawatts and both turbines were near maximum speed to maintain water flow to the boiler. I climbed the 4 steps of the built-in metal ladder onto the front standard of the turbine. I was standing on the oil reservoir and facing the local control panel to do the test.

I was apprehensive about doing the test because you were dealing with a lot of horsepower and if something went wrong, the turbine could trip, and we would lose 50% of the feedwater flow into the massive boiler. Most likely, this would result in the main turbine and generator tripping (doing an emergency shutdown) and losing 550 million watts of power on the grid. This was due to the boiler shutting down, forcing the main turbine and generator to stop.

I overcame my reticence and pensively reached up and turned the thick, steel "T" handle to the LOCKOUT position. This would prevent an actual trip of the turbine. I then hesitantly pressed the overspeed TEST push button. Instantly, the turbine lurched, and the large, high-pressure, inlet steam valves on the left side of the turbine slammed shut with a deep, jarring, metallic thump. The very distinctive turbine whine swiftly decreased in volume as the turbine speed rapidly decreased due to its emergency shutdown.

I was mortified for a moment. I could not believe what just happened. I then turned and, in one large leap, jumped off the turbine front standard to the concrete floor, going momentarily to my knees. I jumped back up in a quick, fluid motion and ran to the nearest paging phone located by the start-up boiler feed pump.

I grabbed the gray handset of the plant paging phone and screamed in total panic, *"START THE START-UP BOILER FEED PUMP! START THE STARTUP BOILER FEED PUMP! START THE START-UP BOILER FEED PUMP!"* After the third time, I cringed, tensing every muscle in my body, waiting for the main turbine to trip. Seconds after screaming for them to start the start-up boiler feed pump, it started, momentarily dimming all the lights in the plant basement. The 6000-horsepower electric motor screamed from 0 to 3600 RPM in about 12 seconds. It was impressive to experience this 6000-horsepower motor roar up to rated speed, dragging the startup boiler feed pump with it.

I listened as the large, pneumatically controlled feedwater valve opened to supply water directly into the feedwater header. A few moments later, the recirculation valve closed with a noise resembling a jet engine shutting down.

I waited in horror for the main turbine to trip. I remained there, squeezing the life out of the handset for about 2 or 3 minutes while anticipating a main turbine trip. I could tell from the high-pitched steam noise in the plant that the main turbine load was reduced, *but the valves never slammed shut.*

I began to realize that my knees ached terribly. I looked down, and my pants were ripped slightly at both knees. This happened as I went down and back up when jumping off the front standard. There was blood oozing from my left knee. I moved both legs and realized there was nothing seriously wrong other than some concrete "rash" and potential bruising. Luckily, I was thin, in decent shape, and only 25 years old. This could have been far worse.

I walked slowly to the elevator and rode to the operating (3rd) floor. I walked cautiously into the control room. Mort Grannitelli and Milton were both there. Mort's face was crimson red. Milt looked angry. Gary Kellogg and Keith Holman were staring intently at the feedwater control panel. I looked up at the red LED MW meter. It was 410 MW. We lost about 140 MW, but the unit was still running. Gary was white as a sheet with a wild look in his eyes and refused to look at me.

Conversely, Keith looked directly at me, squinted, and with venom in his voice, said, "You dumb shit."

Mort Grannitelli looked at me with gritted teeth. "What the hell just happened?"

I tried not to show my embarrassment, but my voice was noticeably shaking as I replied, "I was testing the overspeed trip on the boiler feed pump turbine, and it actually tripped."

"Did you follow the procedure and lock it out?" His voice was tense, his face was growing redder by the moment, and his fists were clenched.

"Yes, I did everything properly. The feed pump turbine is screwed-up. It was not my fault."

"You know we only test the overspeed monthly and then only on weekends when the load demand is down. How will you explain to Bert why you tested it tonight?"

He was right. I now had a serious problem. I looked straight into his eyes, "I will handle Bert. Right now, I am going to write a maintenance request to have the overspeed mechanism checked." I was trying to exude self-righteous confidence when, in reality, I was sick to my stomach and terrified that I may have just finished what I started with the Mike Sciorra incident. Frankly, I was so scared of getting fired that I was about to soil my pants.

Mort walked over and slapped Keith Holman on the shoulder. "You should thank Keith for saving the unit. He did an awesome job!" It wasn't like Mort to compliment anyone. It surprised me.

I walked over to the feedwater section of the control board. Gary still would not look at me. I then looked at Keith and said, "What happened up here?"

Keith shifted from the angry mode and reverted to his usual, snide self as he said, "The boiler feed pump turbine overspeed trip alarm sounded, and Gary hauled-ass to the feedwater board and was about to start the start-up boiler feed pump when I grabbed him and put him in a bear hug. I told him you were just screwing with him." He looked at Gary and laughed. "About that time, I saw the feedwater flow dropping fast and heard you screaming to start the start-up pump. I grabbed the switch, started the start-up pump, and told Gary to open the feedwater control valve 100%." Keith pointed his finger at the trend charts located over the feedwater board. "The drum level was falling fast, so I disabled the drum trip and ran over and tripped "D" pulverizer and then dropped the valves on the turbine to shed some load."

Mort chimed in. "He saved the unit and probably saved your ass." Mort wasn't hiding his anger. I was concerned about Mort, but not nearly as much as I was about Bert's reaction when he found out.

I walked into the Shift Supervisor's office, grabbed a maintenance request (MR) form and began filling it out. I knew I must tilt this as righteously as possible. Any perception of horseplay was going to sink me. The problem now? Any way you slice it, horseplay was the reason *I screwed up... Again.* I decided once again that I must keep it honest. However, honesty doesn't necessarily mean telling *everything*, right?

We finished shift turnover with the day shift crew at about 0700, and I went home with a sick feeling in the pit of my stomach. I never said a word to Vangie because I knew I would get an unsympathetic earful. While she couldn't beat me up worse than I was beating myself, I just didn't need to hear it right now. I climbed into bed and prayed that I would "live" through this. I just fell asleep when Vangie came into the room.

"Mark, Mark, wake up." Vangie gently nudged me until my eyes opened. "Bert Donovan is on the phone and says he needs to speak to you, and it's important." A wave of nausea swept over me. I knew I was screwed. I put on my robe and picked up the phone.

"Mark, this is Bert. I hope I didn't wake you." I was impressed that he was concerned about waking me. Bert's temper was usually bad, and I doubt he would have worried about waking me if he was pissed.

"No, that's fine. What's going on?" I was trying to sound like I didn't have a clue what this call was about.

"I need to discuss the boiler feed pump turbine trip and the M.R. (Maintenance Request) you wrote this morning."

"No problem. What can I tell you?" My mind kept repeating, honesty, honesty, honesty. My gut was saying lie, lie, lie. The mind and the gut are sometimes at serious odds with each other.

"Why in the hell were you testing the boiler feed pump turbine overspeed trip when we were at full load?" At least he wasn't going to pussy-foot around with this.

A million answers screamed through my brain. I had to remind myself that honesty is the best policy. "Frankly," I started as confidently as I could, "We have been trying to get Gary Kellogg to relax a bit. We have been afraid he was going to stroke out if anything major happened." I carefully tried to

94

weave the crew into this and not have me sticking out like a sore thumb.

"I checked the logbooks and didn't see where the turbine overspeed was checked as it was supposed to and thought I would do two things that needed to be done... Test the turbine overspeed and try and show Gary that life goes on when something happens." Okay, the gut and the mind are compromised. Everything I said was true except for checking the logbooks to see if the turbine had been tested. I figured I could tell him I must have missed it in the logbook if he said it had been recently tested.

"You make it sound like you knew it was going to trip." His voice had a concerned note in it.

"Of course not! I just knew that when the test occurred, it sounded the alarms in the control room. This would give Gary the experience of something bad happening, and I pre-briefed Keith as to what I was going to do. He was ready to respond if needed."

"It sounds like Keith did an excellent job catching the unit." He paused. "While I don't necessarily agree with your timing, I like the fact that you are actively working to train Gary." His voice turned slightly upbeat. "I also like the fact that you took the time to check the logbooks and saw that the boiler feed pump turbines weren't tested as they were supposed to last month. They definitely needed to be tested." I was reeling. What I thought was a certain death knell turned into somewhat of an 'attaboy'.

I tried to put a humorous inflection on my voice. "I was worried you were not going to see the wisdom of my actions."

"Don't push it." He said bluntly. "We both know that the timing of the test wasn't right. However, finding a problem with the overspeed trip circuit is something we need to know about so we can fix it."

"I agree, it won't happen again." I realized that I was just given a gift, and I better not look a gift horse in the mouth.

"Get some rest and keep working to train Gary." He paused and then continued with a bit of mirth, "Make him as good as you were in the control room." Wow! Not only was I not fired, but I was sort of complimented by a man who was very stingy with any expressions of praise.

I hung up the phone and regained my composure, thanking the Lord for my redemption from what could have been 10,000 times worse. I knew then I must start making better decisions. Unfortunately, it wasn't my last one, nor my worst one.

CHAPTER 10
THE MAN-LIFT FAILURE

Vangie and I were getting deeply involved with the Church. We taught Sunday School and conducted Children's Church. The Church moved from the tiny Parks and Recreation building to an old garage/warehouse on South Street, a block up from Taco Johns. It was a cold, barely habitable facility with concrete floors, little or no insulation, and only a few drafty rooms. The main room was large enough to provide a decent space for a Church service. Unfortunately, we (the congregation) couldn't afford anything nicer.

We procured an old van and started a makeshift bus ministry. I would drive the 'bus' into Black Mountain Village and retrieve trailer kids. We are not talking about the large, nice trailers like the Basin Electric employees lived in. We are talking about kids who were bounced from town to town in travel trailers, small motor homes, and, in a few cases, even campers. These humble abodes were farther back in Black Mountain Village. This was the area that frequently experienced cop cars racing in with sirens blaring.

While a few of the itinerant kids seemed relatively well taken care of and well-adjusted, most were very guarded with empty eyes. We could get some of them out of their shells, but most were very closed.

In one case, we had a young teenage girl living with her severely alcoholic dad. We received a troubled call from her one evening. She was crying, saying she was cold and hungry. Vangie and I went to the tiny travel trailer and saw they lived in squalor. Apparently, her dad did not come home a few days earlier. The trailer ran out of propane and was cold, and she had no groceries. We picked her up, fed her, and took her to our house, contacting social services.

Using 20/20 hindsight, we should have just kept her. As it turned out this was not her first turn in foster care, and she apparently had bad previous experiences. Vangie and I cried for a full day over her and her situation.

A few days after she was placed in foster care, her dad apparently returned and found she was in the state's care. We have no idea how he learned it was us who retrieved her and turned her over to the state. However, he called, drunk, and spent over 30 minutes explaining how he was going to kill Vangie, our kids, and myself one at a time to show me how it felt to lose my family.

I would hang up, and he would just call back. Frankly, I was scared, but I also knew he was extremely inebriated. This went on for about 2 or 3 hours before he quit calling. I didn't go to the police because I had little confidence in the Wheatland Police Department due to my earlier dealings with them.

Fortunately, I never heard from him again. I found out he worked for B&W, the boiler company installing the boilers at LRS, but was fired for his substance abuse issues. About a week after all of this we noticed his camp trailer was gone from Black Mountain Village. We never heard another word about him or his daughter. This was not an uncommon occurrence as construction continued at the plant.

The plant start-up activity continued to increase. Unit – 2 was finally up and running about a year after the start-up of unit – 1. This is an amazing feat when you consider that 10,000 construction workers were there at the peak of construction. There were three more large transmission lines finished prior to unit – 2 coming online, so we were no longer experiencing a black-plant as often as in the early days of unit – 1's operation.

A few weeks after unit – 2 became relatively dependable, unit – 1 came off-line for its first-year inspection and overhaul. This was a big outage because they were required to correct design errors and repair several bad situations with faulty equipment and components.

Unit – 1 pulverizers required their roll-wheel pressure frames to be replaced because of a flaw causing them to crack. These frames were large, weighed several tons, and required rigging to remove and replace them. This necessitated removing the first-floor stairs in the northwest corner of the boiler room.

These stairs were right next to the man-lift and the elevator. The man-lift is a vertical conveyor belt with small, 14" footplates that you stand on accompanied by handholds. The platforms and handholds were spaced about 10' apart. Each of the 14 floors was equipped with a man-lift platform where you could step on or off the man-lift. LRS is the only plant I ever saw or worked at that used a man-lift.

When you stepped onto one of the small footplates on the man-lift and grabbed the handhold, you would ascend or descend at a relatively fast velocity up or down the towering boiler room. The man-lift never stopped. It was a simple, continuous, vertical conveyor belt. You just stepped on the upward-moving platforms on the south side or off the downward-moving platforms on the north side.

The issue with the man-lift was the obvious question of safety. When you were ascending or descending the boiler room on the man-lift you were unprotected by walls, safety straps, safety belts, lanyards, or anything. You could look down to the basement as you rode all the way to the top of the over 200' tall boiler room. It was just your feet standing on the small moving platform and your hands holding a small handle. If you fainted, or if your hands slipped off the handle, you would be in free fall to the next platform or possibly from platform to platform until your shattered, bloody corpse reached the concrete basement. I don't think this ever happened to anyone, at least not while I was there. I know it was always on my mind when I rode it up or down the boiler room.

The bottom line is that you use the elevator if you are squeamish about heights. You used the elevator if you were carrying tools, a lunch box/bag, or anything else. If you were exceptionally large, you used the elevator. Both hands must be free, and there could not be anything hanging off your body because when you were on the south side of the belt and going upwards, each landing was equipped with a large funnel, making certain you entered the landing without hanging up on anything. The hole at the top of the funnel was not huge. *Stay with me, I am going somewhere with this.*

I was no longer on Grannitelli's shift. I was working with Bob Sturgeon. He was a smart, methodical Shift Supervisor. He never left the Shift office. He was an office man and a true administrator. His two Assistant Shift Supervisors swapped daily between the scrubbers and the main plant each night. Regardless of whether you were scrubber or main plant, you were his legs and eyes. You stayed out in the plant. I loved it. I was not an office person. I enjoyed being in the plant. Bob came to work clean and left clean. We did all the supervising and troubleshooting in the plant. He stayed in the Shift Supervisor's office.

It was our final graveyard shift, and things appeared to be running smoothly on unit – 2 when we took the shift from the afternoon crew. I experienced the usual giddy feeling, knowing that it was our final graveyard, but I learned to quell my desire to do stupid things, or so I thought…

Things were quiet until about 0200 in the morning. With little warning, unit – 2 tripped because the Control Room Operator allowed a pulverizer to start plugging. Being inexperienced, he removed the primary air flow control loop from AUTO and manually added far too much primary air to try and unplug it. It worked too well. His actions rapidly cleaned the mill out and blew a large amount of coal and "fines" into the furnace. This caused the furnace pressure to spike upwards as the large blast of fuel hit the furnace.

In this case, the fans remained operating, but the boiler experienced a Master Fuel Trip (MFT) due to excessive positive pressure in the furnace. I was just entering the control room when I heard the main turbine valves THUMP as they slammed closed. It was an all too familiar sound. Between the shakedown period on unit – 1 and now unit – 2, we experienced a huge number of unit trips.

I ran into the control room and helped the Control Room Operator ensure the unit shut down safely and properly. I always taught my operators that immediately after a trip was a critical period to ensure the plant was brought to a safe condition. Because it was an operator error compounded by sloppy tuning of the boiler control system, we made the decision to immediately restart the plant. I helped get the furnace purge started.

Once the purge was complete, you had 5 minutes to establish a stable flame in the furnace, or the furnace would trip again requiring another purge. Each pulverizer was equipped with seven burner lines to the furnace. There were 7 pulverizers, so there were 49 burners split between the front and back of the boiler on three different floors about halfway up the boiler. Each burner line has an igniter fired with fuel oil that must be inserted into the furnace and lit to provide adequate heat to ignite the pulverized coal stream as it enters the furnace.

You would think that if you already had a hot furnace and inserted ignitors that sprayed a fine mist of air-atomized fuel oil, it would be easy to light. In fact, you would think it would be tough to NOT get them to light. Talk to any plant operator anywhere. Getting ignitors to light and stay lit was a total pain in the butt at most power stations.

That morning, the start-up proved more daunting than usual. We could not get the ignitors to light or stay lit. We were trying everything. Hot restarts were a point of pride and competition between the crews. There was an honor and bragging rights if you succeeded with a quick turn-around after a trip.

Unfortunately, we weren't winning any awards that morning. The oil guns were far more finicky than ever. After about 30 straight minutes of failing to get the ignitors lit, I did a furnace inspection and saw that the pressure in the oil guns seemed way off. The return oil pressure regulator for unit – 2 was on the bottom floor of unit - 1, in the boiler area.

I ran (literally ran) down to unit – 1 and went to the return oil regulator. Getting over to it was difficult because of all the pulverizer parts and other overhaul debris on unit – 1. Unfortunately, I didn't bother calling the instrumentation techs because I felt they were union hacks that would stretch a job out just for the sake of stretching it. Sure enough, upon arriving at the return oil regulator, it was clear that it was not properly doing its job.

I opened the cover to the pressure controller, adjusted it, and then held my finger against the bellows to keep the return oil valve from oscillating. I called the control room on my radio and told them to try the ignitors again. I kept my finger in the controller to ensure the return oil regulator was doing its job properly. I wasn't trying to repair it; I was just working around it.

After several minutes, the control room called and said four rows of ignitors were successfully burning. I noticed it stopped hunting when I took my finger off the bellows. Apparently, once there was sufficient oil flow at the burners, the controller stopped oscillating and appeared to be controlling. I was super-excited as I slammed the door shut on the controller and ran over to the stairs to the control room.

The stairs were gone. They physically removed the bottom flight of stairs to move the pulverizer roller frames to the north side of the boiler. I looked over at the elevator, and it was on the 6th floor because operators were working on the burner decks. This left the man-lift. I ran up the steps to the bottom floor landing but just missed a platform. Rather than waiting a ridiculously long time (about 5 seconds) for the next platform, I simply grabbed the bottom of that platform and let it carry me to the second floor. Yes, I was hanging from the platform by my hands. *No problem...* When it got to the second floor, I swung off and ran up the rest of the stairs to the third floor.

I stayed in the control room for the remainder of the restart. We rolled the turbine, started a pulverizer and then synchronized the generator to the grid. By 0630, when the next crew began dragging in, we successfully brought the unit up to 150 MW, and we were working to get it to 500 MW. I was proud of myself. I went home happy because it was my final graveyard, and I did my job effectively and well. I was ready to sleep for a bit.

I was not in bed for more than a few minutes when Vangie came into the bedroom for what was becoming a reoccurring nightmare.

"Mark, wake up." She shook my arm. "Are you awake?"

"What's wrong?" I opened my eyes, squinting, trying to see her in the darkened bedroom. "Is something wrong?"

"Dallas Wade is on the phone and says he needs to talk to you immediately." Dallas Wade was, of course, the Plant Manager. I grabbed my robe and picked up the phone.

"Mark, Dallas Wade here. You need to come back to the plant right now. We have a serious issue." As with before, his voice was stern and terse, and it scared the hell out of me.

"I will be there shortly," I replied. I honestly wasn't sure what was wrong, and I was especially concerned that he was having me come back to the plant. I knew there was not the slightest chance this could be a good thing.

I arrived at the plant and went straight to his office. It was déjà vu all over again. Bert and Gordon King were in his office along with a union steward and the two night-shift instrumentation people. The union steward was Rob Klement. He was a particularly nasty man with no regard for anything remotely connected to management at the plant. His eyes were always bloodshot, and he bore a course, reddish complexion. He looked like a flaming alcoholic to me. However, I was never near him enough to determine if his eyes and complexion were from drinking or from just being a consummate jerk.

As I walked into the room, it was quite apparent that this was not a social call. EVERYONE in the room looked tense as nails. Dallas led things off.

"Mark, we have a serious problem here. I am going to ask you a couple of questions, and I would appreciate absolute honesty." He glanced at Rob before staring straight back at me. "Did you perform maintenance on the unit 2 return oil pressure regulator this morning?"

I realized then the techs must have seen me at the return oil regulator controller. I decided to be bold and forthright.

"I didn't fix it, I just helped it out in doing its job so we could get fires back into the unit – 2 after our trip this morning. I didn't wait for the instrument people to troubleshoot and fix the controller because we were losing pressure in the boiler." I took a gulp of air and continued. "I wrote a maintenance request to fix the return oil regulator and put this information on the MR." I then stopped and looked over at the two techs.

One of them put his head down and sheepishly looked at the floor. I then continued. "We were unable to get fires back in, and I just steadied the output of the regulator so it would control long enough to allow us to light the oil guns."

Dallas looked over at the instrument techs. "It appears you have valid grounds for your grievance." He then looked square at me through squinting eyes. His facial features were as tight as a drum. "Did you ride the man-lift by hanging from a platform?"

I thought for a moment but once again knew that I better stay 100% honest. I looked straight back at him and said, "Yes, I did. The stairs are gone on the bottom floor due to the outage, and the elevator was on the 6th floor. I just missed a man-lift platform and, without thinking, grabbed the passing platform and jumped off on the second floor and used the stairs to the third floor." Now, it was my turn to look sheepishly down at the floor.

Dallas looked at Rob and the two instrument techs and said, "Gentlemen, please excuse us. We will deal with Mark's safety violation now." He looked back at me angrily as he finished his sentence, "Mark didn't contest your statements." Dallas appeared miffed that I told the truth about the man-lift.

As they were leaving the office, Rob glared at me and said, "You can't be a beacon if your light don't shine." This was an apparent reference to a country western song from a gal named Donna Fargo. My temper instantly spiked, and I wanted desperately to flip him off or tell him what a jerk he was. Luckily, I kept quiet and remained as expression-free as possible.

After closing the office door, Dallas looked at me with chagrin on his face. "Mark, this is truly the most egregious error you have made to date. I can't excuse either of these infractions. Your childish impatience is costing us money to pay the grievance filed by the instrument technicians, but the man-lift incident is entirely inexcusable." He looked at Bert and raised his eyebrows before continuing. "We have to do something to show the plant personnel that we do not and will not tolerate ANYONE, *especially* supervisory personnel, working or acting in an unsafe manner."

I was hoping Bert would come to my rescue and say something about throwing stones or some other homily to save my job but he remained unusually silent. I knew I must act, or I was leaving the office unemployed. Frankly, I was terrified and completely exhausted at being in this situation again.

"Could I make a suggestion?" I asked, trying not to sound pathetic or pleading.

Dallas looked exasperated as he said, "Go ahead."

"I need this job and have tried hard to do the best I can. I realize I have been prone to childish mistakes like this, but I am working hard, really hard, to clean up my act. I was just excited about finding the problem and getting fires back in. I wasn't being malicious…" Dallas cut me off.

"Doesn't matter!" He raised his voice. "You must understand that you are not above the law as a supervisor. You *are* the law and have the responsibility of representing the entire cooperative with your actions." He paused and shook his head. "I have to make a very difficult decision here."

I then cut him off mid-sentence, "Could you demote me back to control room operator?" My voice was now pleading, even though I tried to avoid sounding desperate. "It would be a strong stand against what I did, and I would still be employed in a position that I previously did well..."

Bert then interrupted. "Dallas, I think this is a decent idea..."

Dallas snapped back, "Bert, we agreed that you were going to abide by my decision on this matter."

I now knew I was screwed. This must be why Bert kept quiet up until now. They apparently already argued about me over this latest mess. Bert looked at me with fire in his eyes and, with a noticeably shaking voice, barked, "Mark, go to my office and wait for me there." I didn't say a word. I just left Dallas's office and went to Bert's office, praying under my breath that I didn't get fired.

Things must have been even worse than I realized. As sound-proof as these offices were, I could still faintly hear yelling coming from the corner office. The rumor mill continuously circulated that Bert and Dallas did not get along because Dallas was so much younger than Bert. I don't know if there was any truth to this or not. I wasn't privy to their day-to-day interactions. I do know that Bert went out of his way to protect me again.

I was sitting, wilting, in Bert's office, praying under my breath that I would not be fired, when Bert finally came into the office and shut the door. "Am I unemployed?" I asked quietly with an air of hopelessness.

"Very, very close." Bert seemed exhausted. I never saw this side of him before. "You are not getting demoted or fired, at least not yet. You are getting a full week off without pay. This will be well advertised in the plant, and you are on probation for two full years." He raised his eyebrows and looked directly at me. "If you have even the smallest infraction, issue, grievance filed against you, ANYTHING at all, you will be immediately terminated without recourse. This is a done deal. Even the slightest infraction… *There won't even be a meeting. You will be escorted off the plant site.*"

I knew then that during the 30 minutes in Dallas's office, Bert fought valiantly for me. There was no question that Dallas had already made up his mind to fire me, but Bert went out… *Way out* on a limb, once again, to save my job. Why? I don't know. Maybe he saw a little of him in me when he was young? Bert could be impetuous and impatient, but he was fully competent. In fact, he was one of the best powerhouse men I ever knew. Whatever the reason, I will always be indebted to Bert for what he did for me.

The oddest part of this is the fact that about 20 years after these events, Bert would work for me. If someone had told me this in 1981, I would have laughed out loud in their face. I could barely stay employed, let alone find myself at a point where I would hire Bert. Sometimes, life is filled with crazy ironies.

CHAPTER 11
THE DISNEY WORLD DREAM

I now knew I was on a short leash and couldn't do **ANYTHING** further to screw up my job at Laramie River Station. I became extremely careful with everything I did and said at work. My paranoia was off the chart, but it was working because I was not getting into any trouble. Everything I did was rolled around in my brain at least twice and then not completed unless it was 'by the book' or at least by the union contract.

Because of this, the passage of time slid into a continuous, excruciating loop. Dayshifts and afternoon shifts went quickly, and graveyard shifts would agonizingly grind me into exhaustive submission. By the time the last graveyard shift rolled around, I was convinced that I already died and was living in hell. However, I tried my hardest to stay employed and not do stupid, mind-numbing things.

At least Church was good. We were learning more every week and getting further involved. A Church is a living organism that attracts birds of a feather. I didn't understand this then, but years of Churches and Church experience have provided a profound understanding that people will flock to familiar or comfortable circumstances. The problem with this is simple. The definition of familiar or comfortable circumstances varies by personality and person.

Some Churches are filled with downers. People who can barely hold their heads up. Some Churches are filled with givers. Some are filled with takers. Some attract the garish and loud, and some attract the quiet and introverted. Is this a problem? Not usually. If the Pastor/Minister is balanced and teaches properly, a Church's goal is to make everyone better and not worse.

In my opinion, the true goal of a Church is to bring people to the understanding that we are flawed people. All of us. Zero exceptions. The Old Testament clearly documents early history and shows that there were none righteous, not even one. Yes, this is a scripture. But it is true. It was true back then and is true and observable now. Every other religion beyond Christianity teaches how to become better.

Christianity teaches that everything is based around love and forgiveness and that we all need, *NO*… We all desperately *REQUIRE* forgiveness. Christ paid this price for our ultimate forgiveness. When we truly wrap our heads around this, it makes us want to become better because of His sacrifice and teaching of love and forgiveness. Unfortunately, Churches can be some of the worst for not understanding love and forgiveness.

Chan Bayne's Church, OUR CHURCH, fragmented and broke apart. I was surprised and disappointed by the rapid collapse of Alliance Faith Chapel. To this day, I think Chan is a great guy, an excellent Preacher and Pastor, but some don't. For the most part, Chan Bayne pastored a very spiritually mature and knowledgeable group. Vangie and I were not one of these people. We were on a vertical learning curve and knew there was a massive amount we did not know. However, many of the people in Chan's Church were very knowledgeable and… *Critically nit-picky.*

In 20/20 hindsight, I think many of the people in Alliance Faith Chapel wanted to be the Pastor and felt more than qualified to do so. When you attend a non-denominational Christian Church, you are subject to many people who truly feel they are called by God to Pastor the Church more than the Pastor. It is an occupational hazard that Pastors confront regularly. Anyway, Alliance Faith Chapel, sadly, died.

Upon the demise of Chan's Church, we migrated with the Marquettes to the Assembly of God Church. Bob Little and his wife were pastoring it. Bob was a 60+-year-old construction worker and a very 'down to earth' man. He spent his life in the construction trades and knew what a lay person on the job in a blue-collar position dealt with.

His best sermon I ever heard was proving that we are flawed from birth. He spoke of a baby that starts crying in the crib to get attention, but not necessarily because of a real need. It sounds overly simple now, but you needed to be there. It was truly a great sermon.

He gave another good sermon about raising kids. He discussed how some parents say they are going to leave the choice of going to Church to the child's discretion when they are 8 or 10 years old, but the same parent(s) will insist the same child wear a coat outside if it is cold. His premise was a simple one. You insist they wear a coat when it is cold, but you let them decide what could be the most important decision in their lives. Bob did a good job from the pulpit. We enjoyed Church there, and it helped break the monotony of working and living in Wheatland.

I filed our 1980 income tax return in early February of 1981. I was excited because we were getting a sizable chunk of money back. This money, coupled with ample vacation time, convinced Vangie and I to do something special with the kids. I called a travel agent and discussed the possibility of going to Disneyworld in Orlando, Florida. She did some investigation and came back with a very attractive package that would be fully covered by the money from our income tax return. Vangie and I were excited and, after some discussion, called the travel agent and booked the trip. We, of course, never did anything like this before and were exhilarated that we could make this trip.

Not long after booking the Disney World trip, I experienced another seemingly prophetic dream. In the dream, I saw Vangie, Brandi, Brittanie, and I in Disneyworld. The dream was very clear and not as surreal as many dreams can be. It began with me walking into the Shift Supervisor's office at LRS. Bob Sturgeon and the Shift Supervisor of the previous shift were there.

Bob looked at me and said, "Milt called in sick, so you must cover both the scrubber and the main plant today. It sounds like they are having some problems in the scrubber, so head out there when you've completed shift turnover." The dream, then, instantly shifted to a new venue.

I saw a large airport and the 'Welcome to Orlando' sign, presumably in the airport. I then saw us having an amazing time in the theme park. I clearly remember the smiles on the kid's faces. The dream then sequenced back to the airport. We were in the boarding area, and the flight was delayed.

I walked to a boarding area window and looked at the plane. It was an Eastern Airlines jet. I was a bit confused in the dream because it looked like a 737 but wasn't a 737. I knew a little about aviation because of flying with Wylie as a kid and my love for mechanical things. I knew the difference between the major jets and was noticeably confused because the jet did not quite fit the description of what I knew to be a 737.

The dream continued as I watched the mechanics remove the cowling off the starboard engine (right side). They appeared to be working on it, which wasn't a good sign. The gate agent then announced that the flight to Denver was being cancelled due to a mechanical issue on the aircraft. She said to remain in the boarding area so they could rebook the passengers on other flights.

A short time later, the gate agent came back on the public address system and said they were moving us to another gate very close to the current gate as they found another available plane. Everyone began migrating to the new gate. As soon as we got to the new gate, they announced that we should return to the original gate because they were able to repair our jet.

Everyone then slowly migrated back to the original gate. The realism and clarity of this dream were stark. I remember looking back out the window at the jet and seeing the mechanics closing the engine cowling. In the dream, a chill went down my spine.

We then boarded the jet and taxied to the runway. Once on the runway, the pilot put full power on the engines, and we accelerated to lift off. As soon as the nose went up on the jet, I looked out the plane window and saw the starboard engine burst into flame. At the same time, the plane rolled steeply, and I felt the wing contact the ground. We crashed. I then saw a glowing human figure in the sky with his arms open and Vangie, the kids, and I moving towards him, hand in hand. I immediately awakened with a start.

I lay in bed, confused and emotional. I just saw myself and my family die in a fiery plane crash. It did not end violently in death but in us moving towards a figure that I felt certain was Christ. It was still very stressful and emotional. I could not go back to sleep for over an hour.

I got up and walked into the front room, praying, asking the Lord if the dream was from Him. No answer, at least not that night. I finally went back to bed and fell asleep.

The following day, I awakened tired still reeling from the dream. I decided I could not say a word to Vangie until I determined whether it was real. I dressed and went to work. After getting to the plant, I pensively entered the Shift Supervisor's office. Bob was already relieving the graveyard shift supervisor.

As I walked into the office, Bob looked at me and said, "Milt called in sick, so you must cover both the scrubber and the main plant today. It sounds like they are having some problems in the scrubber, so head out there when you've completed shift turnover."

I went completely numb for a moment. His words staggered me, and the entire setting was exactly as I saw and heard in the dream. There was no difference whatsoever. None. I just stood there trying to comprehend what was happening.

Bob looked back at me. "Are you okay? You look like you just saw a ghost or something."

"I'm fine." I was stunned and reeling as I was still trying to process everything.

"Seriously," Bob looked at me with concern as he continued. "You are white as a sheet. Are you feeling okay?"

"Yeah, I'm fine. I will check out the scrubber after shift turnover." Everything blurred as I sat down to relieve the graveyard supervisor.

The rest of the shift was surreal, as I was dazed and confused. I knew I saw our deaths. There was no question. This *WAS* going to happen. The check and balance, or proof, was the incident with Bob at shift change.

It was not a coincidence. Had it been a normal shift change, there might be some doubt. However, Milt called in sick, and everything was word for word. What was said in the dream was just too much to be even remotely considered a coincidence. Plus, when I experienced the dream about Larry's death, it used the same format of showing me something that happened the next day and then showing me what was to come. This now seemed a standard in my "prophetic" dreams. I would see something relatively insignificant that happened the next day, and then the remaining portions of the dream would come to pass.

I got home that afternoon and sulked around the house. I cried when I picked up Brandi and Brittanie. I hugged them like I never hugged them before. I knew I must enjoy them as much as possible in the time remaining. This made me cry again. Vangie was irritated because I would not tell her what was wrong.

I told her, "Nothing, I just have a headache," and continued to brood with my thoughts going in every direction imaginable.

Should I *NOT* take the vacation after all? My mind was abuzz with confusion and contrary thoughts. Was this a warning, and I still had time to fix it? Was it inevitable? If I pulled the plug on the vacation, what would I tell Vangie? Thoughts of fear, anger, sorrow, and even apathy spun wildly through my mind and heart. I told Vangie my head was really hurting, and I was going to lie down.

Once in the bedroom, I continued to reason and make sense of why God would show me this. I could not come to any conclusion. I decided that maybe the scene in the Shift Supervisor's office was a one-in-a-trillion coincidence. I knew it wasn't. However, this thought kept me sane.

The next several weeks were very difficult. Vangie couldn't understand why I was "acting differently." I was constantly hugging and playing with the girls and trying to show a lot of love to her. What she was seeing was me being depressed and trying to hug her a lot. She continued to ask why I was so down. I would then work as hard as possible to act 'normal' again.

I secretly wrote a will. I didn't leave anything to Vangie and the kids because they were going out with me. We didn't have much, but I gave most of it to Wylie. The problem was that the house and the car were both mortgaged to the hilt. We really didn't have anything other than furniture and household goods, and we certainly didn't have any savings because I still sucked at money management. I didn't realize it then, but I simply left Wylie an obligation to clean out our house when we didn't return.

Finally, our vacation to Disneyworld was upon us. After 3 weeks of being morose and depressed, I decided why not enjoy this vacation as much as possible? *I realized that the advantage of living each day as if it were your very last was truly appropriate in this case.*

Heck, I reasoned that I was missing a full set of graveyard shifts and would never have to do them again. This made me happy. I did not have to worry about money because, at the completion of the trip, I was relieved of ever paying bills again. We could spend money like there was no tomorrow and thoroughly enjoy ourselves without worry, right? After getting my mindset right, I promised myself this was going to be the best vacation anyone could ever have!

We drove to Denver from Wheatland and then flew from Denver to Orlando. There was an early spring snowstorm that I thought would keep us from going on vacation. For several hours, I thought there was a glimmer of hope that we would not actually go to Disneyworld. Nope, we were able to get to Stapleton International Airport in Denver and the flights, while delayed, were still flying.

The vacation package included round-trip airfare on the now-defunct Eastern Airlines. Our jet was a brand new one that looked just like a 737 but wasn't. I asked what it was and found out we were flying on an Airbus A-300. According to the gate agent, Eastern Airlines leased several jets for $1.00 from a relatively new aircraft company in France called Airbus. Airbus agreed to the lease to break into the American market. A market that was dominated by Boeing and McDonnell Douglas.

As it turns out, Eastern Airlines liked them enough to buy them. We were flying on an A-300 Airbus. At this point, I knew beyond any shadow of a doubt the dream was true and final. There was no way I knew about Airbus A-300s in my dream. I just knew I saw an aircraft that was like a 737, but not a 737. It was *this* aircraft. I now knew that we could throw caution to the wind and do whatever we wanted on this vacation because I would never be faced with paying the bills for overspending.

The package included staying at a Days Inn hotel near Disneyworld. Whatever we wanted to eat, we ate. Whatever we wanted to do, we did. I do not believe for a moment that anyone ever experienced a more carefree vacation than we did on that trip to Disneyworld.

At one point in the theme park, Vangie looked at me and said, "I was worried about you being grumpy or depressed on this trip because of the way you have been acting. I am so glad that whatever was bothering you is not doing so now. The kids and I are having a fantastic time."

This made my day. I was still carrying the burden of knowing we were never returning to Wheatland, but I could not say a word to her about this. We just continued to enjoy ourselves as much as possible.

After several days of carefree fun the trip wound down, and we were back at Orlando airport. The burden of our upcoming deaths was now strangling the life out of me again. When we arrived at the departure gate, I looked out on the tarmac and saw our jet. It was an A-300 Airbus. It was the jet I saw in the dream.

What's more, mechanics were working on the starboard engine. I went numb for a moment. This was it. As I stared at the plane, Vangie interrupted my moment of shock.

"Mark, watch Brandi. I am taking Brittanie to the bathroom." I looked at her, trying to contain my out-of-control emotions. As soon as she saw my face, she asked me, "Are you okay?" She had a look of intense concern on her face. "You look terrible. Are you sick?"

"Yeah, I am fine. Take Brittanie to the bathroom." She continued to stare at me for a few moments.

"Do you need an aspirin or something?" Her concern was genuine. She was digging in her purse to get an aspirin for me. This was typical Vangie. She knew how to take care of everyone and was always equipped to do so.

"I'm fine, honest. Take Brittanie to the bathroom." She slowly shook her head at me with a look of concern and then left the departure gate area for the bathroom. I was shaking and felt uncomfortably cold. I picked up Brandi and gave her a long hug. She squirmed a bit because I was clutching her so hard. I then sat her back down and just stared at her. She was such a beautiful child. Vangie returned from taking Brittanie to the bathroom just as the gate agent made an announcement.

"Folks on Flight 138 from Orlando to Denver, we just received word that they have cancelled this flight due to mechanical issues with the aircraft. Please remain in the gate area so we can help rebook everyone on another flight."

It was exactly like my dream. I even knew what was going to happen next. It had to. Everything to this point progressed precisely according to the dream. Why wouldn't it continue? Sure enough. After a bit, the gate agent announced, "passengers on flight 138 from Orlando to Denver, I was just informed that we have located another aircraft. We will now

120

be departing from gate 11 instead of gate 9. If everyone in the boarding area would please move to gate 11…" I stopped listening. My mind trailed-off to the ending of the dream.

"Wait here," I told Vangie slowly. "I need to go to the bathroom."

"You really look terrible. Are you sure you're okay?" She asked again with even more concern.

"I said I'm fine, I just need to go to the bathroom. Just wait here until I get back." I realized I snapped at her. Rather than apologize, I just turned and walked to the bathroom straight into a stall. I was shaken to my core. I decided to pray.

"Lord, should I not get on this plane? I know what is going to happen. Did you show me this to save our lives?" I started to weep. I was sick to my stomach and thought I might throw up. I cannot fully explain what happened next. Peace inundated me. The peace that passes all understanding settled gently upon me. Total, complete peace. My stomach quit hurting, and I quit shaking. In fact, I felt warm, like I was wrapped in a thick blanket. I stood in the stall for several minutes praying but not really saying anything. The peace was real, and it was overwhelming.

I went back to the boarding gate. Vangie looked at me and said, "You look much better. Did you throw up?" There was reason to ask this. Anytime I ever turned completely white, I would usually throw up and feel better.

"No, I just went to the bathroom. I feel much better." My voice was firm. It must have put her at ease.

"We need to get to Gate – 11." She said as she took Brittanie in her arms and grabbed the diaper bag. "Get Brandi, and let's go down there."

"It's not necessary," I replied quietly. "They are going to fix our airplane."

"How do you know that?" She asked incredulously.

"I just know."

She stared intently at me, scrunching her eyes as she tried to figure out what was happening. She and I were exhausted from the pace we kept on this trip. I think my revelation on the repair of the airplane irritated her.

"Well, until they make an announcement, we need to go to the gate – 11." I acquiesced, and we walked to the new gate. We were only there for about ten minutes when the announcement came that our plane was repaired, and we should return to gate – 9. The gate agent was very apologetic for the inconvenience.

"How did you know they were going to fix our plane? Did you hear someone talking in the restroom?" She seemed a bit wary and confused. I knew I couldn't tell her anything. However, I was still feeling total peace.

"I just knew," I answered, allowing my voice to trail off as I took Brandi's hand and started toward the original gate. Vangie followed me, still looking confused and a little irritated.

I looked out the window at the gate – 9, and sure enough, they were closing the cowling on the starboard engine. It was still exactly like my dream.

It was another 30 minutes before we boarded. We were afforded early boarding because of the kids. It allowed us to get to our seats and settle in. We were on the aircraft's starboard side, just like in the dream. I put my head back onto the headrest and closed my eyes. I still felt peace and wanted to say goodbye to Brandi, Brittanie, and Vangie, but I knew it would freak them out. I just acted like I was resting my eyes. Tears were squeezing out from my closed eyelids and slowly running down my cheeks. I turned my head towards the window to keep Vangie from seeing my emotions.

The plane finished boarding, and the door was closed. We taxied out to the runway. I had a knot in my stomach but was holding it together due to the peace that was still upon me. With my eyes closed, I whispered a short prayer.

"Lord, I give you Vangie, myself, and my kids. Thanks for the blessings you have given us." That was the prayer. *Nothing fancy or dramatic.* The A-300 engines spooled-up, propelling the large jet aggressively down the runway. As the jet's nose went into the air, I garnered every ounce of courage possible to open my eyes and watch the engine explode. However, our altitude continued to increase, and eventually, the pilot reduced the throttle, and we leveled out.

The engine didn't explode.

We didn't crash.

The flight continued uneventfully to Denver.

Why? I don't know for certain. I do know this moment changed my life forever. It had been changing for a while, but this changed me at the very core of my being. Maybe it was a test. I just don't know.

There will be naysayers writing this off as bluster, exaggeration, or simply *coincidence*. However, the odds of this happening randomly would be mathematically impossible to even calculate. It doesn't matter. My life was changed forever after this experience, and it would never again be as it was.

What I didn't realize then was an incredible, specific plan for our future was already in-place and later would be unstoppable. *I couldn't fathom now just how much our lives were about to again, change.*